Here Lies My Heart

Here Lies My Heart

ESSAYS ON WHY WE MARRY, WHY WE
DON'T, AND WHAT WE FIND THERE

A Beacon Anthology

Deborah Chasman and Catherine Jhee, Editors

BEACON PRESS · BOSTON

BEACON PRESS
25 Beacon Street
Boston, Massachusetts 02108-2892
www.beacon.org

Beacon Press books are published under the auspices of
the Unitarian Universalist Association of Congregations.

04 03 02 01 00 99   8 7 6 5 4 3 2 1

This book is printed on recycled acid-free paper that contains at least 20
percent postconsumer waste and meets the uncoated paper ANSI/NISO
specifications for permanence as revised in 1992.

Text design by Christopher Kuntze
Composition by Wilsted & Taylor Publishing Services

Library of Congress Cataloging-in-Publication Data

Here lies my heart : essays on why we marry, why we don't, and what we
    find there / Deborah Chasman and Catherine Jhee, editors.
        p.   cm. — (A Beacon anthology)
     ISBN 0-8070-6217-0 (pbk.)
        1. Married people—Psychology.   2. Single people—Psychology.
    I. Chasman, Deborah.   II. Jhee, Catherine.   III. Series.
    HQ503.H48   1999
    155.6'45—DC21   98-39975

Contents

Foreword

W E M A R R Y to find safe harbor in a roiling, roaring sea. We marry to avoid gray loneliness in a small room with only a hot plate and a thin cat. We divorce to find ourselves, and free ourselves of self-defeating templates of childhood misery. The chasm that separates us from a partner terrifies us; the prospect of intimacy does too.

I am one of the married, and one of the divorced. I believe in luck, more than I did the first time (then, I believed, mostly, in me) and I believe in the efficacy of psychological hand-to-hand, a real effort at monogamy, judicious candor, and a sense of humor, but I believe that even all that works only when built on good sex and a deep, even unfathomable, affection for one's spouse. The nature of marriage, the end of marriage, the impossibility and necessity of marriage are the favorite topics of almost everyone. This group of twenty is no different:

just more articulate, more honest, more provocative versions of ourselves.

There are the sensible demurrals of Katha Pollitt (who skewers statistics as the empty pages they are), the reasonable solutions of Barbara Ehrenreich (let's stop expecting good daddies to be great lovers and vice versa), and the passionate bleakness of David Mamet matched (perhaps for the only time in their literary lives) with the bleak passion of Cynthia Heimel. The mournful, intelligent insensibility of Phillip Lopate not only persuades us that marriage is "a long patience" but he makes us feel how long and how patient one must be. Cal Fussman takes on a final, macho adventure, through darkness and knife-bearing strangers, to prepare him for the true adventures of marriage's unknowable territories and glittering vistas.

The voices of Rebecca Walker, Marjorie Ingall, Joel Achenbach, Amy Hempel, and Kate Jennings give us actual people behind our modern photo albums, such as a purple-haired bride; a single, skeptical woman at the family gathering; a proud young father, heavily teasing and secretly grateful; the happy, slightly secretive smiles of a younger bride and much older groom.

We have our honest, smart, older, and wiser adulterers, in mid-flight, in sad descent, in poignant recovery, in Gerald Early, Louise DeSalvo, and Lewis Buzbee.

Willie Morris and Mark Doty explore the end of marriage, but not of connection; the end of life, but not of love, both writing from the heart, holding the soul of the past.

Nancy Mairs and Edward Hoagland walk us, with such elegant style and such grievous brutality through the making of one marriage and the unraveling of another, that we cannot help but notice that the line between Stay and Go is disturbingly narrow and shifting, in a life together.

Through Vivian Gornick's pensive eyes, we not only remember loneliness, we see it, and when she holds it to the light, we now see beauty where we have only seen a dark craquelure.

And if you believe that happy marriage is possible, that for some lucky people the beautiful "mended garment" can be torn and patched with love and regret, cruelty and forgiveness, read the final essay, by Lynn Darling. And if you don't or can't believe in happy marriage, read Darling's essay twice.

This book is for the once, never, and much married. For believers and skeptics, love's fools and love's thieves. It is for people with long memories and long histories and for people who reinvent themselves in every new town, new decade, new relationship. This book is for everyone whose heart lies where it should, where it shouldn't, and, in the end, where it must.

Healthy, Wealthy, and Wise

WHY DID you get married? Was it to boost your savings rate? Lengthen your life span? Protect yourself against risky behaviors like driving too fast and getting into fistfights? If you're like me, you probably can't give a coherent account of your decision to marry. You may even be paying a therapist large sums of money, thus lowering your savings rate rather drastically, to explain yourself to you. But now, thanks to Linda J. Waite, professor of sociology at the University of Chicago, you can put that checkbook away. "Does Marriage Matter?", her paper at the Population Association of America's annual conference, sets out the benefits of wedlock with such enthusiasm that it won't be her fault—or that of the media, which have trumpeted her findings coast to coast—if the nation's aisles aren't trampled beneath the stampeding hooves of brides and grooms.

Marriage, Professor Waite has discovered, is good for you. Married people have more money, more sex, more satisfaction and, as previously noted, longer lives than singles or cohabitants (actually, her tables show cohabitants have the most sex, but her text elides this inconvenient datum). Married people live in safer neighborhoods, "experience an orderly lifestyle," and have children who are less likely to drop out of school.

None of this is exactly news. After all, if marriage didn't hold out powerful advantages, why would anyone wed? Certainly we don't need sociology to tell us that two people pooling their resources and facing life together can reap benefits unavailable to those who are single or who live together but keep their resources separate. This would probably be true in any society, but is particularly the case in America, where for millions of people, marriage is the only social welfare system: It is how they obtain health insurance and pensions, help with the kids, and a roof over their heads. From the legal system to Thanksgiving at Grandma's, Americans shower approval on marriage. As any advocate of gay marriage could tell you, Waite's big revelation is actually a buried tautology: Marriage confers upon John and Jane the advantages society accords to married people.

Everyone understands this. That's why, despite oceans of social change, the rate of white women who've never married has hardly budged from around 20 percent since 1950—a fact Waite obscures by stressing the rising proportion of never-married black women, a tiny percentage of the adult female population, whose never-married status is largely a function of declining numbers of marriageable black men. So who, exactly, does Professor Waite think needs to be sold on marriage in the same urgent spirit in which doctors campaign for exercise and against smoking?

She writes as if the nation were teeming with anti-marriage zealots, women (naturally) who "see the traditional family, balanced on the monogamous couple, as fundamentally incompatible with women's well-being." But, in fact, the people fleeing marriage are the people who've tried it. And it's a funny thing; Waite's own statistics suggest there's something in that feminist critique: The benefits of marriage are notably skewed. Men report greater physical satisfaction in sex within marriage; for women, marital status makes no difference. Unmarried and divorced *men* are the ones with the noticeably increased risks of heavy drinking, and it is men who derive an income "premium" from marriage or cohabitation. For women, the negative health effects of nonmarriage are fairly trivial, and marriage, which boosts men's earnings, lowers their (unless, interestingly, they're black). The downside of the "specialization" of roles Waite calls a plus to the married couple is the wife's second shift: housework, child care, husband-mothering.

For a scholarly paper, "Does Marriage Matter?" uses some rather odd data. Chart 5, for example, "Being Unmarried Is More Dangerous Than Heart Disease," comes from a 1979 article in *Health Physics* by the physicists Bernard L. Cohen and I-Sing Lee, who included

unmarriedness in a whimsical list of ordinary life conditions that were more dangerous than nuclear radiation,
about which they felt people were foolishly concerned.
The home of this factoid, then, lies somewhere between humor and propaganda. I enjoyed Cohen and
Lee's proposed remedy for fatal singlehood, though:
government-run computer dating services. Perhaps, as
an added inducement, Newt Gingrich could come
across with some of those honeymoons in space he likes
to talk about.

The truth is, social science is not much help to the individual trying to chart a course through life. The cate-
gories are too crude, the numbers too big, the causal
connections too suspect. You might indeed be healthier,
wealthier, and wiser if you married—but what if your
suitor was O. J. Simpson or Al D'Amato? Instead of
touting marriage's practical advantages, Professor Waite
might more usefully have asked why half of all married
people nonetheless forgo them in favor of studio apart-
ments and an early grave. Waite lists the usual reasons for
the "decline" of marriage—women working, changing attitudes toward nonmarital sex, etc.—but these
explain only why divorce and cohabitation are possible, not why people embrace them. Could it be that the
prospect of spending the rest of your life with someone
you don't love, maybe don't even like, is so painful that
plump investments and balanced meals pale by comparison?

The troubadours, who argued that love and marriage
were incompatible, since marriage was an economic

and social arrangement and love was adoration and passion, would have had no problem understanding the
marital instability Professor Waite finds so perplexing.
To her Ben Franklinish case for marriage as a matter of
prudence, prosperity, health, and convenience, they
would reply, *The world is ablaze with possibility and—mon
Dieu!—you speak of savings rates? Of someone to nag you
about your smoking?* I don't know about you, but I'm with
Bernart de Ventadorn.

Why It Might Be Worth It (to Have an Affair)

Q: SANTA CLAUS, Darth Vader, Batman, the Perfect Man, and the Perfect Woman are driving along together when they suddenly get a flat. Who changes the tire?

A: The Perfect Woman, of course—the others are make-believe characters.

In the folklore of gender relationships, love is something wild and crazy, while marriage is sober and sane. But the folklore has it backward. All we want from love, after all, is everlasting, unqualified adoration, preferably accompanied by lifelong bliss. But for purposes of marriage we demand something far harder to find—the perfect, all-purpose Renaissance man.

Think about the roles we late-twentieth-century women expect a husband to fill. He should be a co-provider and a reliable financial partner; a co-conversationalist and sparkling dinner companion, fully briefed by CNN. In the event of children, we expect he will further develop into a skilled coparent with a repertoire of bedtime stories and remedies for runny noses. He should be prepared to jump into sweats and serve as a sturdy fitness partner, plus handling home repair; a husband who can't locate a fuse box is about as useful as one of those little plastic tool kits from Toys "Я" Us. And since we are modern women, we have every right to think he will manage, in addition, to be a tireless and imaginative lover, supplying orgasms virtually on demand.

It reflects well on us as women that our expectations are so varied and exacting. A generation or so ago, a woman counted herself lucky to find a good provider; it was a bonus if he didn't beat her or drool in his soup. Only as women became breadwinners, too, could we begin to expand our demands—throwing in sex appeal in the late '60s, coparenting in the feminist '70s, financial partnership in the fiscally challenging '90s. As for home repairs: Well, women aren't home all day anymore, baking casseroles and waiting for the plumber to show up.

We've earned the right to expect multifaceted perfection in a mate. The only trouble is, it doesn't make sense. Why should a guy who's good in bed also be gifted at bedtime stories? Or a fellow who can drywall a basement be a scintillating dinner-table companion? No one expects her pediatrician to come over and prune the shrubs, or her accountant to fold laundry and put the kids to bed. Only in marriage do we kiss common sense good-bye and expect that every single human need can be met by a single all-too-human being.

So we lurch from marriage to marriage, doomed to perpetual disappointment. If numero uno was a safe corporate workaholic, numero due is likely to be an un-employed poet with a taste for jug wine, or vice versa. We feel betrayed—yes, betrayed—when a freshly ac-quired husband reveals some basic klutziness in any of the myriad departments he's supposed to excel at. In short, we wrecked the institution of marriage by ex-pecting too much from it. We loved it to death.

Now maybe it's time to cut the spouse some slack and put more of our demands on the rest of the human envi-ronment—in other words, to rebuild the ancient and honorable notion of community. How about friends for some of those long talky dinners? Extended family to help with the kids? Clever neighbors to turn to when the basement floods? Or, for that matter, the occasional studmuffin for a sexual fling? Not that husbands—and wives—shouldn't try to excel on all these fronts. But clearly, if marriage is to survive as an institution, they need reinforcements.

Between Men and Women

W HEN ALL is said and done it is, of course, always about sex. What else could it be about? And if it is constantly changing, what else could it do?

Cheap entertainments record or counterfeit the sexual act, but that does not get to it, or it only satisfies us to the extent that we deem sex entertainment.

The lawyers say it starts in bed and ends in court; and, indeed, the contemporary barrage of pornography is counterbalanced by our brave litigiousness.

Drama or music can provoke a near-sexual appreciation in exciting a love of death. Many seek and live to sustain this feeling, as if one could live in abandonment forever—it is the adolescent equivalent to the search for perpetual motion.

The child tries to square the circle, thinking, "Many have failed, but I am blessed"; men of more advanced age set out to conquer the world, the land, a skill, one or some women.

And women, for their part, what would they be painting and primping for if not to conquer that same man?

Where, in this seamlessness, is there room for misery?

In the yearning for romance, in the man's Mariolatry and in the woman's hero worship, is the urge to conquer and the urge to subdue in the ironic operations of chance upon the enthusiastic, in the bitter and protracted conversation of remorse.

We are crazed to get into it and crazed to get out of it.

We are unbalanced by passion or by the hatred of the passionate.

The only control seems a dry unregarding philosophy, practicable only by those pitifully devoid of such gifts of spirit as our own.

We find our misplaced passions ludicrous, but not our hatred; and our new painful wisdom, in the termination of the marriage, the affair, the pact, or the illusion, frequently finds that new partner of such proverbial unworthiness as to send our friends scurrying for the telephone.

Through it all, as audience or actor, we nod our heads sagely, or shake them in sorrow, and know that in spite we are fated to square the circle, come at the Hesperides, and live both happily and forever.

But who would want it if it came to us?

In both demands we are as the infant—center of its world—who requires that the world conform to both and each of its two modes: furious and satiated.

And, of course, at the same time, we call it grand.

The chance discovery of the old love letter, the personal erotic code, three words or symbols on a florist's card, the note found in a coat unworn these years since the end of the affair that came to a bad end; the anger, the self-loathing, the embarrassment, are confusingly sharp, as are the souvenirs and memories of more successful love—both relics of decision and folly proved by time to've been operating in service not of our own personal dreams but of the mating instinct. There is its stamp, even in the curses of the divorce court, the sex slanders of the popular press, the lawsuits and totalitarian sexual proclamations of freedom: "You have disappointed me. I demand you, your sex, someone, be all-in-all to me, and you have failed. Redress my wrongs, make me complete"—the one sex demands the other make it whole, and even the supposed dry legalistic debate is nothing other than a simulation of the sexual act: "Complete me, release me, make me whole." What a surprise.

And the women can confab with the women and the men herd with the men, as both have always done, and bitch to each other without end, but to consider such affinity other than a counterbalance is to confound the racing form with the race.

The former can have final interest only to those who have not seen and do not long to see the horses run.

What could be more lovely than two folks in love, more sordid than two bickering—that demand that not only their partner but the community make them complete, as if one were, for all the world, returning a defective item to the place of purchase and exhibiting its shortcoming. As one is. For it was the group that gave us our choice, and if we are, as we are, not fated for bliss, then surely the group, in large or small, must bear the fault.

We love the wedding, but we adore the divorce. Its entertainment value is protracted through the rift, the threat of reconciliation, the legality and postmortem recriminations.

The wedding proceeds with thoughtless speed from the courtship (in itself a bore to any but the two) to the ceremony and then to the community's wait for, and insistence upon, the first offspring.

But no, we, speaking as principal, exclaim, nothing, not birth or parenthood, neither wisdom nor age, will debar us as participants in the drama of sex.

We will claim until death at the very least the honorific right of search for bliss.

Why with one rather than another?

The figure, or the face. Their intellect, or wit, or this-or-that—we fall inevitably back upon "a certain, indisputable something" proclaiming them the one. But how often has that something led us astray—like a compass that is sure of north, but whose north bears no relation to any known pole. And yet we believe in it, while kindness, courtesy, and their sure indications of potential happiness beg for believers.

But through much of it we have no goal, only a desire for a state—that state that would amalgamate the thrill of the hunt with the torpor of perfect repletion. What a laugh.

I suppose we could strive to maintain our dignity, and some of us do, and most of us do at some time.

That dignity might rest on a sense of humor and, for the odd instance, an appreciation of tragedy and perhaps some belief in its curative powers.

At the end of the day we want someone to hold our hand. If we are happy we want someone to be a hero for us and someone to whom we can be a hero. In misery we strive to be or find a victim.

In either case we're searching for a partner to share our idea of home.

It Takes a Hell of a Man to Replace No Man at All

I HEAR YOU GOT married," said a long-absent ac-
quaintance I ran into at a party.

"Six years ago," I said.

"Well," he said, momentarily nonplussed, "let me be
the last to congratulate you!"

But he was not the last. I am congratulated often—I
congratulate myself often—on the choice I made, a
Southern gentleman I first described to friends as having
no ax to grind and nothing to prove.

I married late. I was twice the age my mother was
when she got married. When I told my two younger
brothers that I was getting married, they said to my future husband, "We don't know whether to congratulate
you or *thank* you."

My family never pressured me to marry; this was a

great gift. It probably prevented a training marriage. My friend Terese, who had two training marriages before the one that took, says finding a good husband is about "luck, patience, and endurance—like scaling Everest." She says she realized she had chosen the same man each time, "but each time with slightly better tailoring—the Calvin Klein approach to marriage."

Another thrice-married friend feels herself, with each succeeding husband, to be on "a sort of Indian spiral toward Nirvana." A good husband, she feels, has a good sense of humor, "someone who can carry on when the dark is dark—it's the only human attribute we have with which to cope." And, she adds, "he should have few addictions. Who'd want someone with *no* addictions?"

My most-married friend says that husbands number one and four were the same, and two and three were the same. (The sonnet approach to marriage? A-B-B-A.) "One and four were both dominant, aggressive, and powerful. Two and three were both passive, submissive, and touchy-feely. I was like, 'If that didn't work, maybe this will.' They were all good in some ways, but flawed." I asked her to free-associate on the words *good husband*. She is a psychotherapist who has examined her experience at length; she said, "What comes to mind is something I've never had. It's why I keep moving on. I'm an adventurer. I've never been with an equal adventurer. Or someone with a grasp of what brings me joy."

My friends are glib—"Are we talking about sexual performance? Pulling in the big bucks?"—or dully earnest, speaking of maturity, respect, and sharing the weight. My own feeling about a good husband sounds like a country-and-western song: It takes a hell of a man to replace no man at all. I prized, and continue to prize, my solitude. It is a necessary condition of my work. The women I know don't talk about financial support when they talk about their husbands; the support we require is psychological, so we can continue to have our own lives.

Are you a good husband? I asked a newly married friend. He told me he had overheard his wife singing a French song she had learned from her mother. "The only line I could make out was, 'A good husband fits in an apron pocket.' She wouldn't translate the rest."

Beware of Mr. Right

I HAVE RUN away from home. I threw some clothes into a suitcase, grabbed the dogs, got in my truck, and drove to San Francisco. Now I have checked into a hotel. I am really frightened. Whenever I go outside I keep falling, bumping my head on trees and poles. I keep going blank.

The city is too much to cope with. Homeless people frighten me. Dead-eyed rich women madly shopping frighten me more. Victorian houses painted mauve with orange trim make me think I'm in Pennsylvania, hallucinating. I am not myself.

I can't decide what to do about my wedding ring. Put it on, take it off, repeat for an hour. It's such a beautiful ring, from Tiffany's, too expensive, too elegant.

I married one year ago. It was so perfect. My husband and I became friends on the phone first. He led me to believe he was a fat, ugly, soft, pasty computer geek, so I thought, OK then, friends. When I first saw him, in the parking lot in front of the bookstore where we were to meet, I thought, damn, what a gorgeous, brawny construction worker. If only he had brains.

Three weeks after we met he was to pick me up at the airport. I got off the plane and saw him standing there in the terminal with a huge bouquet of red roses and a tiny blue box. I got dizzy. He led me to a chair in the waiting room, got down on his knees, and proposed marriage.

"Yes," I said, yes, oh, absolutely yes, I want to be married to you, my wonderful dream man. No more confusing connections, no more nausea brought on by doomed expectations. You are smart, you are totally hilarious, and you are beautiful. Absolutely. There is no doubt about it. Yes.

Today is my birthday. My friend Bey got a party together fast. I wore my wedding ring. All these lovely San Francisco friends, saying, "Happy birthday! Where's that darling husband of yours?" I made up bright chirping lies. I put on a paper tiara.

I didn't marry him for money, or for fear of becoming a lonely old maid. I can't wait until the day I am an old maid, trolling through the Oxfordshire countryside with a pack of dogs and a wicked tongue. I was not only content on my own but often downright festive as well. Then I fell in love with this man all the way to my reptilian brain.

We laughed and laughed. We squabbled over shelf

space and forced each other to read favorite books. In the supermarket he liked to grab me and start fox-trotting. We each thought the other was madly sexy, even as I was putting on weight, then more weight. And got headaches. My cholesterol count rocketed out of control. And we laughed and laughed.

Yesterday I left the hotel and drove into the country, to a tiny town at the edge of California. A hotel was the marriage counselor's idea. "When it gets like that, pick up your purse, go to a hotel," she said. The driving for seven hours was my own twist.

How do marriage counselors sleep at night, knowing all they know about marriage and not screaming it to the world? They should stand on their rooftops in their pajamas with megaphones, shouting, "Citizens! Heed my words! Never marry! Marriage is bad! Marriage is a bloodbath!"

But no, everyone keeps mum. No one tells you about the sniping in the kitchen, the words like grenades flung across the bed, the radioactive silences in the rose garden. It's a big state secret that the merest ghost of a grimace of disapproval can cause cold-blood rage.

My husband and I looked right into each other's souls and felt the urge to kill each other. I don't know why. I don't know how I ended up locking myself in the bathroom and puking into the toilet for the sake of love.

When I see into a beloved friend's soul, I am full of affection, forgiveness, acceptance. But a beloved friend doesn't shriek with abandonment fear when you start to walk out the door. A beloved friend watches calmly as you go away for days or even months. A beloved friend shows no interest in scrutinizing your every action for a clue to some sort of secret betrayal.

It's the sex, of course. Primordial-ooze sex, the people's choice.

The conspiracies of the selfish gene make the machinations of the military-industrial complex look like a game of ticktacktoe.

I decided when I was in the cardiologist's office and the technician was pasting electrodes all over my body that perhaps this marriage wasn't working for me. My reptilian brain had come up with a sudden new agenda: Get the fuck out, now.

So I have rented myself a little cabin with a record player and actual thirty-year-old vinyl records. Right now I'm listening to The Band sing "The Shape I'm In." I feel OK. Well, awash with grief, but no longer insane and a danger to myself and others. I have walked on empty beaches, staring at the shark-riddled ocean. I have discussed my life with the ospreys and the night herons, who are good listeners.

Women have, of course, taken over. They're feeding me, massaging me, giving me acupuncture and Chinese herbs, finding me places to stay and telling me to start crying already for God's sake or I'll never feel better.

Men have stayed politely in the background, the pharmacist solicitously filling my prescriptions, the mechanic silently changing a flat tire with a "she could blow at any time" demeanor.

My jeans are loose; I am healing nicely. As soon as I'm better I am going to drive back into the city and get myself a honking huge tattoo of a snarling canine alpha bitch.

I can't wait to show my husband.

Empathy-Challenged and Proud
Why I'm incapable of feeling your pain

I AM THINKING a lot about empathy these days—defensively, I might add—because my wife, Anne, keeps accusing me of lacking this quality in relation to her. Of course, I readily agree. I sympathize with her pain but stop short of empathizing with it. My saying this infuriates her even more, and she is the kind of person who has no shyness about retaliating. I explain that what feeble mechanism I might have for empathy is nullified when I'm attacked: I cannot identify with a person who wishes to cut me to ribbons. That is my imaginative limitation.

At what point, I wonder, did the word *empathy* begin to displace *sympathy*? *Empathy* isn't even in my 1971 *Oxford English Dictionary*. This may reflect the more reserved character of the British; one assumes the rage for empathy began on this side of the Atlantic. (See Bill Clinton's "I feel your pain.") The most recent edition of the *American Heritage Dictionary* tells us that while sympathy "denotes the act or capacity for sharing in the sorrows or troubles of another," empathy "is a vicarious identification with and understanding of another's situation, feelings, and motives."

To me, sympathy suggests a humane concern for others' positions or plights, based partly on a generalized ethic of compassion for all living things. Empathy conveys, to my mind, a more sticky, ghoulish shadowing that stems from the arrogant delusion that one can actually take on, or fuse with, another person's feelings.

It is possible that my wife wants to recapture that sense of romantic communion, usually strongest during the infatuation phase, when lovers' hearts are said to beat as one. But I can't help suspecting she got this empathy bug after a session with her therapist, Larry.

Since then, as a result of our frequent bickering and my wife's conviction that her therapist is a marvelous person, we have entered into couples counseling with Larry. To my surprise, he is a marvelous person. Wise, reasonable, scrupulously evenhanded, and empathic— perhaps to a fault. Sometimes, when he commiserates about the pressures we are operating under—raising a three-year-old with health problems while juggling our careers—I begin to wonder about this warm compassion, the depth of which, it seems to me, ought to be reserved for Romanian coal miners, not yuppies like us.

In one session, we were recounting a disagreement

we had had the night before. As it happened, about sex. We had been going through a dry spell, mostly because of my wife's preoccupation with our baby daughter and mistrust of my capacity to empathize with her. Now she said she was getting ready to consider doing it again, and I replied, like an idiot, something to the effect that I'll believe it when I see it.

Larry offered an alternative script, giving us the lines that, in his view, we might more profitably have spoken. I was to compliment her on making this overture to an advance, and if I still needed to express skepticism, she was to show that she understood my feeling "vulnerable" because I'd been starved for sexual affection. Larry then asked what I thought would happen if Anne had replied that way. Feeling the old obligation to speak the truth in therapy, I took a deep breath and said that his suggestions had nothing to do with life as it is lived; that he was trying to indoctrinate us to talk the new, totalitarian Empathy Speak.

"Are you really against empathy?" he asked, somewhat incredulously.

"I am, yes—"

"You see?" Anne said. "You see what I have to put up with?"

I went on to say that I was for sympathy, that old-fashioned term. The people I admire most, like two friends of mine, both in their seventies, operate out of a moral code older than empathy that acknowledges that the gap between two souls can never be entirely bridged. Nor should it. I thought of my old professor,

Lionel Trilling, who questioned D. H. Lawrence's hunger for total honesty by saying: "Why should two people have no secrets from each other?" On the other hand, there is much in the present culture that promotes an exaggerated or false empathy, like the figure of the talk show host, the Great Listener—Oprah or Geraldo—whom I consider dangerous.

As you might imagine, this did not go over well. I saw that my attempts to explain myself were perceived as inappropriately "academic," therefore cold, removed from emotions and the business at hand. (Interesting that therapy today has that anti-intellectual edge. This is no place to start thinking.)

When people start speaking of reason as a "defense," I get nervous, considering where the irrational has taken us in this century. And, grateful as I am for Larry's willingness to help straighten out our problems, I can't help watching my tongue now in counseling sessions. I have a lingering suspicion that couples therapists train you to say not what you genuinely feel, but what is less confrontational, all the while telling you that they want you to be in touch with your feelings. They want you to make nice.

I suspect I will never be able to empathize with the panic and depression my wife sometimes feels—for the simple reason that both terrify me too much. I grew up far too close to such emotions in my parents, and it took all my strength to distance myself from their debilitating pull so as to form a workable, reasonably cheerful self. Where does that leave the marriage? My wife still hungers for a more empathetic soul mate, while I am equally convinced that I am realistically offering something else that is of value. Call it an understanding of limits, based on the intractability of human nature and the intensely problematic—not to say tragic—dilemma of modern marriage.

Given my empathy-challenged situation, I am faced with the choice of trying to fake an empathy orgasm— a distasteful proposition—or waiting out my wife's rage, hoping that in the end she will come to accept my defects, as I hope and pray to accept hers. Forbearance, resignation, and stoicism still seem to me the only way to go. Someone once said, "Genius is a long patience." I don't know about genius, but I would maintain that marriage is a long patience—at least when you're committed to making the marriage last.

Going to the Temple

How does a purple-haired, tattooed, nose-ringed feminist get married? It sounds like the setup to a pigboy Rush Limbaugh joke. But it's what I'm trying to figure out.

I was never the kind of girl who had wedding fantasies. I never sketched wedding dresses in my notebook or wrote my hoped-for married name over and over in flowy, smiley-face-over-the-i cursive. (Vomit.) When I grew up, I met a succession of boys who were fun to sleep with. I even fell in love with one, but I wasn't ready to think about spending the rest of my life with anyone. Anyway, he was kind of wussy.

Then I met Jonathan. Reasons why I love Jonathan: Never bores me. Loves Eeyore even more than I do. Beautiful, big, strong hands. Owns every issue of *Sassy*. Has eyes like the sea after a storm. Grows daisies and sunflowers for me. Lots of chest hair. Does interpretive naked dance around the house after a shower. Sings "la! la! la!" like Pee-Wee Herman. Amazing cook (hardly ever consults recipes). Always, always puts the seat down.

We started as friends, and did that sneaky, irresistible build into love. It took my tiny reptilian brain a while to figure out I was a goner. Now I reread our e-mail from back then and can only shake my head at my delusional, unconscious flirting technique. I would tell him about the postcoital habits of female praying mantises. The very first thing he said after we finally slept together, I kid you not, was "If you want the children to be named Ingall, I'm fine with that."

He was my first serious Jewish boyfriend. My mom was plotzing with joy. Two weeks after we moved in together, Hanukkah came and we lit the menorah together. Neither of us had ever done that with a lover before. We said the blessings with goofy tears in our eyes. Finding each other was a miracle. We'd lived on the same street in college but never met. Then we moved to opposite coasts and met through the wonder of e-mail, and pixels began to dance on the screen.

We're already living together, so why get married? Because I know what I'm getting (the aforementioned good stuff, plus temper tantrums, inability to hang up shirts after wearing them, black sulks, narcissism, offsides use of the phrase "Cut it out, you're acting like my mother"), and want to spend my life with him anyway. I want to acknowledge this in front of our family and

friends, in our religious tradition. We're not kids; we
know what forever means. (Oh, god, it means we *never
get to sleep with anyone else again!*) I've heard of weddings
where the couple say, "as long as our love shall last." Um,
no. I want to say in front of everyone that this is holy, and
legally binding, and I care enough about this person to
enter into a very ancient covenant with him. (I think
I'm far from alone in my desire for both community and
continuity. To some degree, I think that's why so many
Gen-Xers are having big weddings. We feel cast adrift
and we want tradition, moorings. Or maybe it's just a
trend, like martinis and lounge music.)

Marrying Jonathan means figuring out how to turn
a patriarchal institution into something that does not
harsh my feminist mellow. Two institutions, really, because marriage is for me inextricably tied with Judaism.
Suddenly I'm thinking about Jewish children, Jewish
household rituals, a Jewish wedding ceremony.

Lately I've been obsessing about the *ketubah*, the Jewish marriage contract. How can I make it reflect my values while still keeping it in accordance with Halakah,
Jewish law? The traditional *ketubah* is a legal document
(it mentions neither love nor God) stating that the
groom has "acquired" the bride for a given price and
agrees to support her. The bride merely assents, word-
lessly. This is pretty darn retro, especially considering
the fact that I've been the primary breadwinner for the
last year. Our *ketubah* will have Jonathan and me each say
that we will support the other. Instead of the Orthodox

business of having the *ketubah* signed by two male witnesses, we'll use four: two men and two women. Oh,
and then there's the little business of my dearly departed
maidenhead. We will not be mentioning it.

The fun stuff is pondering the design of the contract.
I first considered incorporating a quote from the Song
of Songs, the *Friends* haircut of *ketubah* quotations—
lovely, yet so common as to totally lack individuality.
Instead, I think we'll use a quote from the blessing said
every month on Rosh Chodesh, the new moon. I love
moon stuff anyway (I am woman! Hear me menstru-
ate!), and the Rosh Chodesh idea conveys the little quo-
tidian miracles Judaism celebrates. A good marriage is
also about the little things. And as I said, I think Jonathan's and my meeting was a little miracle. We could
have met at any time, but had I met Jonathan in college, I
would not have been ready for a grown-up relationship.
We'll incorporate stars and moons into the *ketubah*, to
match the motif I painted on various bits of furniture
around the house. Maybe we'll also put in some sunflowers and tulips, to represent the ones Jonathan grows
for me on our deck.

So anyway, here's my translation from Hebrew of
the Rosh Chodesh blessing: "Grant us long life, a life
of peace, a life of goodness, a life of blessing, a life
of strength and health, a life of piety, a life free of shame
and reproach, a life of wealth and honor, a life full of
love of Torah and fear of the heavens, a life in which all
our hearts' desires for goodness will be fulfilled." A bit
literal, but a good backstory, as they say.

IT'S HEALTHY, I think, to reexamine old institutions and futz with them rather than throw them out entirely. Working for change from within lets you feel connected: turning your back entirely sets you adrift. There's a lot to be proud of in Judaism's attitude toward marriage: Jewish law has always said that minor girls can't be betrothed; that women have the right to refuse any potential husband, no matter what their parents command; that women can sue for divorce on various grounds, including sexual dissatisfaction; that conjugal rape is prohibited. I like that Jewish tradition has the bride and the groom escorted to the *chuppah* (wedding canopy) by their parents; much nicer than having the bride's dad hand her off to her husband like a football. It still blows that in Judaism, men have the power to grant a divorce. Jonathan and I will either put in the *ketubah* that he will give me a divorce if I want one, or we'll have a prenuptial agreement. Kinda icky to be pondering, and I do think this is forever, but better safe than sorry. (Thanks, Ivana Trump!)

Speaking of change from within: my role model is my mom, who is a professor at the Jewish Theological Seminary and the mother of a gay son. She recently spoke to the Rabbinical Assembly, the international body of Conservative rabbis—an august group if ever there was one—about how they needed to be much more welcoming of gay Jews. She didn't say, "Bite me," and become a Reform Jew or a Buddhist. I think she's the shit. I want to keep my name largely because it's hers. (Yes, I know hers is my dad's, and if she hadn't changed it, it would be her dad's. You make your choices and do what you can.)

We all personalize institutions to reflect who we are. For our wedding, I'm planning on keeping my hair purple and rubber-stamping moons and stars on the yarmulkes. Jonathan will smash the ritual glass and preside, tongs in hand, over the barbecue the day before. After the honeymoon, we'll continue in the household roles we forged over the last year: he does most of the cooking, I do most of the cleaning; he gardens, I paint and decorate. I don't really expect marriage to change anything, but in my head it clears the way for having kids, which I'm crazy-mad looking forward to. I'm supporting him now so he can support me when I want to drop out and have me some pups.

A section of the Song of Songs says:

> *Set me as a seal upon your heart*
> *A seal upon your arm*
> *For Love is strong as death*
> *Cruel as the grave*

I thought about using it as a *ketubah* motif. Then I thought about how I could personalize it further. I'm thinking of getting another tattoo, this time of Eeyore. Because Jonathan is the seal upon my arm. I can be so literal sometimes.

How I Bought My Wedding Ring

THE SALESWOMAN warned me. To some men, it's as uncomfortable as a noose, she said. Many wear it only because their woman insists. Once, she'd seen a guy tug so hard to remove one that it flew across the room and lost itself inside the slats of an air conditioner. But that was extreme. Maybe I'd just be like most men who'd never worn a ring before and treat my wedding band like a toy or a musical instrument, spinning it 7,000 times in a day or beating out radio tunes on the steering wheel.

My marriage is young, but I haven't yet twisted, tapped or tugged once. I do find myself staring, though. Sometimes, late at night, I look at the gold wrapped around my fourth finger and see everything: the crashed airplanes, which looked like crushed insects, the morning vapor rising off the Amazon River, the biblical downpour, the fingernails of the second sister sliding

through the hair on my chest, the veins being pulled out
of my forehead . . . the look on her face when my fiancée
said there could be no wedding. The images are locked
in this gold band—and this gold band is locked on me. I
chose a wedding ring that fits so tight it can't come off.

THERE IS no way I could make this story up.

It starts five years ago, when some extremely foolish
words left my lips. I told the woman who'd so joyously
accepted my marriage proposal that I had no intention
of wearing a wedding ring.

Her eyes squinted and her hands slowly settled on her
hips. "What do you think, that I'm going to get married
alone? So you're just like the rest, aren't you? You won't
wear a ring so that when you meet another woman . . . "

"Docinha, rings don't feel comfortable on me. Never
did. Never will. It's that simple. What does a ring have
to do with being faithful, anyway?"

"Safado!" She spat this word at me. "Sa-fa-do!"

I'm not quite sure her meaning can be accurately
translated into English from her native Brazilian Portu-
guese. But I'll try. It'd be something like "You smarmy,
unctuous, hollow-cheeked Lothario, salivating like a
flea-ridden hound in heat."

Was this the woman I'd described to friends as a rain-
bow without the storm? The one I'd met on a crescent
of virgin sand near the equator and had first kissed amid
coconut trees and sea breezes? People back in the United
States laughed when I told them it had been love at first

sight. But I'd been traveling around the world for ten years and had seen about all there was to see. My instincts knew she was perfect before I could blink.

The argument over the ring was our first. Why did I incite her anger? Why go against an honored tradition that has bound men and women since Roman times? It had to be more than physical discomfort. Only now, looking back on it all, can I see that my fear of marriage was much deeper than I could have imagined. The habits formed in a decade of drifting from one misguided adventure to another were not going to die easily. And so the gold rush was the natural compromise between me and the wedding ring.

I'd read about it in a magazine. A single nugget of gold weighing 137 pounds had already been pulled out of a pit called Serra Pelada in the Amazon rain forest, and Serra Pelada was but a mosquito bite of gold. The Amazon is roughly as large as the continental U.S., and there was gold buried all over it. Nearly 250,000 men had swarmed into the rain forest, turning it into a tropical wild West in which claims were being recorded on the back of matchbook covers and illiterates were inking their thumbprint onto the backs of checks worth hundreds of thousands of dollars.

Yes, I told Docinha, I'd wear a ring. She was so happy to hear those words that she didn't seem to mind my idea. I was going on one last adventure before settling down. Into the Amazon—to find the gold to make our wedding rings. And if I just happened to find a little more . . .

From 10,000 feet, the land looked like a salad bowl filled with broccoli. The airplane landed in Boa Vista, a city in the north of Brazil, and I sensed that I had gotten good information when a whore sashayed by on the arm of a man wearing a solid-gold necklace as thick as her wrists. This was the frontier: circular mining sieves, forty-niner–style, were on sale in the streets, and bars were filled with stubbled, laughing, ornery men.

The heat soaked my shirt with sweat, the sky turned an ominous gray, and hotel clerks scoffed at me. The town was overrun with miners, and not a single hotel room was available. I walked for hours, lost. Turning a corner, I came face-to-face with a dog that growled and lunged and nearly bit off the finger on which the wedding ring was supposed to go. As I reeled away, it hit me. What the hell was I doing? Was this trip just a feeble self-deception, a hollow attempt to live with myself after finally caving in to convention?

I got past the dog and asked an old man with a mouthful of gold teeth for help. He pointed me toward a neighborhood of dwellings in which miners paid to hang their hammock, and it was here that I came upon the wooden house with the screams.

They were screams of delirium, completely ignored by the few men sitting around a gimpy-legged table. One of them noticed my curiosity and answered the question on my face.

"Malaria," he said. "Everybody gets it."

He clapped his hands above his ear, then opened his right palm. A bloody mosquito lay dead. He held it out for my inspection. "Only the female mosquitoes carry malaria," he said. "Watch out for the women, just like in life."

João the man's name was, a pilot who flew miners into and out of the forest. Three times, he'd crashed. Four times, he'd survived malaria. He laughed at my story. "All the way from the United States . . . ," he said, shaking his head. "What do you know about prospecting?"

"Absolutely nothing," I said.

There was cackling among the miners, and then we watched the sky crack open. We moved inside and watched the storm. The men were grateful for my presence. Their old stories became as fresh as the reactions on my face. They warned me about the forest, about the twenty-five-foot anacondas that fell out of trees, wrapped themselves around your chest and slowly squeezed the air from your lungs until you were unconscious and could be swallowed whole. They told me how sometimes miners got lost in the forest and never came out and how it was difficult just to get in now, during the rainy season. Often the landing strips muddied and planes skidded as they came down, and crashed. The pilot went into the house and came out with photos of planes looking like the mosquito still on his palm.

The more they talked, the more frightened I got, and the better I liked it.

For the next few days, it went on like this. The rain, their stories, my stories. During a lull in the storm, we went to the airport and looked at the airplanes that transported the miners. Some of them appeared so old

and tiny, I could imagine the pilot yelling "Contact!"
and winding the propeller to get them started. For the
right money, the pilot said, he'd chance a flight. Thunder rocked the earth as he spoke. "I think I'll wait until
it clears up," I hedged.

"You'd better be prepared to wait for a while," he said.
"Rainy season lasts for months."

The wedding was three weeks away. It would be too
much to ask my bride to postpone it.

"Five days without luck and you're disappointed?"
the pilot asked. "You don't have much future as a miner.
Let me tell you about a man who passed years without
luck. Panning, starving, cursing. Then one day, he hit it.
He traded his gold in for cash, put it in a box, went to a
bar, got drunk and started folding and taping his money
together in a chain. When it was long enough, and
when he was drunk enough, he started running through
the streets with the chain behind him. He ran and ran
until he fell down with tears in his eyes, laughing like a
lunatic. Someone asked him why, and do you know
what he said? 'For so long I've been chasing the money.
Now the money's going to chase me.'"

I smiled. "Where did he make his find?"

"South of here, south of the equator." The pilot
stroked his chin. "That's where you should go. It's dry
season there now. They say there are two nuggets there
for every one here."

I CANNOT tell you where I went. My wife, no doubt,
will read this and if she knew, it might mean the brutal
end of three sisters. Not to mention me.

I found a boat heading south on the Madeira River, hung a hammock under the stars and woke to cantaloupe sunrises that made me wonder if I'd ever be able to go off alone like this once I married and lived in a house.

Near the place I cannot name was a small city in which flocks of green parrots skimmed the sky and barefoot boys shinnied up trees to slice down coconuts and townsfolk went to the square in their best clothes on Sunday nights. I stopped at a small shack—the town's cultural center—to stare at a painting. It was the most amazing work of art I'd ever seen. Insects, animals, birds and foliage had been put on canvas in the most intricate detail, yet somehow they all seemed to be melting.

"*Daime.*"

"What?"

"It's a tea made from a certain vine and its leaves," said the clerk. "Some people call it a drug and are scared of it. But not the artist who painted that. He says *daime* holds the mystery of the forest."

"Where do you find it?"

"I can introduce you to the artist."

The artist was going to a place in the forest to drink some in a few days, and he invited me along. To this day, I'm not sure if it was the *daime* that shattered my life or the wait to drink it.

In those few days, I met a young woman, not without charms, who was attracted to me—or to the notion of putting her arms around a foreigner (who can be sure?). I told Tanya right off that I was searching for a wedding ring for my fiancée. It was a foolish thing to do; she, too, could not resist an impossible quest.

"There's no harm in merely kissing," she kept reminding me as she simultaneously worked to keep me away from the admiring eyes of an older sister and a younger one who were not without charms themselves. A fierce competition broke out among the three for the foreigner.

Ultimately, none of them lost.

I WENT TO the telephone several times but could not dial Docinha's number. My head swam. The artist showed up. It was time to drink the *daime*.

As we walked into the forest, he explained to me how the *daime* affected different people in different ways: Some floated into the sky, others descended to the core of the earth. Some vomited, others felt nothing at all. Mostly, he said, the *daime* magnified whatever was inside you.

We followed a trail I could barely discern and came upon a wooden house filled with people eager to share the mystery of the forest. An orange froth was ladled from a pot into a glass, from which everyone drank while a group of young women started singing the first of 127 prayers. By the time the last prayer was finished, the artist told me, the effects of the *daime* would have worn off. I gulped the thick liquid and winced. It tasted like chimney smoke.

The women sang with their eyes closed. Time passed slowly. Just as I was certain that I was one of those people on whom the *daime* would have no effect, I heard my fingertips start to melt. I looked down and panicked. Now my hands and my forearms were dripping away. I tried to gather myself, but my entire body was losing its form, and then two huge hands reached up from the ground, grabbed the veins in my forehead and tugged. My veins stretched like elastic, following the hands that slowly descended into the ground. I ran outside to escape, but the hands would not let go, and my forehead fell to the soil. Deeper and deeper my veins were being pulled into the earth. I turned my head and saw a fly larger than a building greedily rubbing its hands, and diamond raindrops the size of cars crashed all around me, and I hugged a towering blade of grass to keep from being blown away by the cyclonic purple winds whipped up by the fluttering wings of an angry butterfly.

One hundred and twenty-seven prayers can last a long time.

The first thing I did when the artist left me at the hotel the next day was phone Docinha. She was sobbing. "Where have you been?" she asked over the static. "I needed to talk with you. Two days ago, I had to go to the hospital for surgery. I lost our child."

My knees stuttered and I grabbed for the back of a chair. "I didn't know you were pregnant," I said.

It took me days to get back upriver, to fly back to Docinha on the east coast of Brazil. But the scent of all that had passed did not wear off, and Docinha has an acute sense of smell. "Where is the ring?" she asked. I started to tell her everything, but she cut me short. "Can you look me in the eyes?" she asked.

There was nothing I could say. She became very quiet.

"I need to be alone. Go back to America."

"You don't understand."

"No, you don't understand. How do you expect me to marry someone who doesn't have roots, who leaves me with a child, runs off, and has not the slightest respect?" She was crying and steely at the same time. "I need time to think. Please, go back to America. I will call you."

THE MAN who had once wanted to see every place in the world now had no place to go. I didn't want to fly off to the U.S. That would mean losing Docinha. So I decided to travel for a few weeks in Brazil and then return after she'd had time to think.

I found myself on a bus headed to a city called Salvador, sitting next to a man who was blacker than midnight. Erivaldo said I looked worse than death, and I told him why.

"Don't worry," he said. "Your problem can be solved in the city."

That night we arrived in Salvador, a bit of Africa in Brazil, the northeastern port where thousands of slaves were brought centuries ago to work the sugarcane and cocoa plantations. We wound our way through darkness, over dirt streets, past shanties and outhouse odors and black women with long faces staring curiously out of window frames without windows, until we came upon the chanting, candlelight, shadow and smoke.

"What is this, voodoo?" I asked.

He laughed. "We call it *candomblé*."

We stepped inside the house. Erivaldo disappeared, and then I saw the glint of a knife.

The man gripping the knife nodded solemnly to me. The knife came down. A chicken began dancing a samba without its head.

Erivaldo found me backed into a corner. He led me through the dancers and chanters into a candlelit passage, toward a thin black woman wearing a white dress and turban. The way she sat made her chair seem like a throne. Stones glittered from rings on almost every finger.

She motioned for me to kneel, then ran her fingertips over my palms, up my arms and over my face. They lingered on the veins in my forehead. "It is a very strong curse," she said.

"What can you do?"

"I will make an offering. But this curse will not be gone soon. Remember this: You are a son of Xango, God of Iron and Thunder. Look to him and he may help you."

And that is all she said. The next day, I phoned Docinha. When she heard my voice, she hung up.

I returned to the United States, my pants still speckled with the blood of a sacrificed chicken.

DAZED I WAS, waiting for Docinha to call. But the days passed, and the call never came. I wrote to her but received no response. I phoned her. Her phone number now belonged to someone else. I called her office. A man said she'd been transferred to another city, but he didn't know where.

"It's over, can't you see?" a woman friend of mine chided. But I could see only Docinha. I'd pass a Brazilian club and imagine her dancing, pass a beach and want to kick in a wall.

The months went by. "You're crazy," said a male friend. "She's probably married by now."

Then it was a year, and I met another woman. Blonde, sweet, good-looking, smart, American. Her parents liked me. My parents liked her. I kept writing to Docinha.

There was no response. The brother of the blonde woman was getting married, and I was invited. The affair was held in early November in the Midwest. During the reception, one of the blonde woman's friends asked me about my travels. I told her that I'd spent time in Brazil, that I'd nearly married there.

"Well, aren't you glad that it didn't work out," the friend asked, "so that you could be here with us tonight?"

I wanted to punch this woman. But I excused myself politely and walked outside. I looked up at the sky and remembered the night in Salvador and Xango, God of Iron and Thunder. "Okay," I said aloud. "If I can get her back, I want to see a sign. I want to hear thunder, to see lightning. Right now."

There was no rain within the surrounding four states. I stood in the parking lot and stared at the sky for ten

minutes . . . fifteen . . . twenty. The night was so clear
you could see to the edge of the universe.

"What's the matter?" It was the blonde woman. She
took my hand. "C'mon, everybody's dancing."

As we walked to the hall, I kept my neck craned to the
sky. Nothing. I swallowed hard as we walked into the
room where the band was playing:

> *It's like thunder, lightning,*
> *The way you love me is frightening.*
> *Better knock on wood, baby. . . .*

I started to laugh, to laugh and laugh and laugh, and
when the blonde woman asked me why, all I could say
was "I love a god with a sense of humor."

I phoned Docinha's office. She answered. Her transfer, it turned out, had been temporary. Her hello
reached out and hugged. Then she realized it was me,
and her voice turned suspicious, like a border guard's.
She said she had work to do and couldn't speak long.

"Just one question," I said. "Are you married?"

There was a long pause. "No."

I began to write to her every day. I told her that I was
ready to put down roots. *If it takes you fifty years to believe
this, then I am prepared to wait.* It took her only a few
months. When I stepped off the airplane in Brazil, we
embraced as if we'd never been apart.

Not long afterward, we were on Fifth Avenue in New
York City. In a jewelry store there, we chose our gold
bands, much like everyone else.

Serial Lover

My stepmother frequently asks me, usually as I am recounting my latest travels and most current loves, when I am going to get married. "What you need," she says, tilting her head and looking deep into my eyes, "is to settle down, to stop all this moving about and make a home for yourself." I don't think she cares who or what sex my partner will be, or whether or not our union is legally sanctioned, she just wants me to make some long-term vows, and promise myself to a way of life for the foreseeable duration. She calls that "marriage." To her, marriage and life partnership indicate stability, maturity, coming to terms with one's wants and needs, commitment to one's life path. She can't imagine that all my "exploring" might boil down to something greater than hedonistic escapism. On rough days, when I long more than anything for a social script to tell me what to do, how to behave, how to love, who to be, I wish that my inner wiring, the encoding of my DNA, was so simple. Find your work, find your mate, find your house, find your Self. If only the road to realization was so straightforward!

Even after five "long-term monogamous relationships," the alchemy of a new relationship still exerts a mysterious pull on my psyche, leading me, heart first, into heady, swirling waters. Inevitably "it" appears in my life when and where I least expect it, a perfect template cooked up by my unconscious and my lover's, showing up at an appointed time as if by magic. The relationship, that thing that is neither s/he nor I, but some living amorphous form created by us both, opens another door. Under my lover's gaze and in his or her arms I feel myself change, open, flower. In this new territory, I am free to create myself again, to explore unexplored facets of my psyche. Here, with each new person, I open myself wider, and learn how to love and be loved better than ever before. When there is trust and caring and open communication, a willingness to tolerate discomfort and still keep going, old hurts can be healed, new words spoken. I cease being the self I knew and become the self that I have been moving, ever so slowly, toward.

When friends and family speak to me of marriage, of being together forever, I bite my tongue and wish them happiness, but secretly wonder how on earth it can be found within such a configuration of limitation and restraint. Marriage seems to me a perfect metaphor not for opening doors and plumbing uncharted depths, but for closing gates, surrounding and fencing in primal emotions like need and especially fear: fear of loss, fear of change, and even fear of death. Marriage feels like the ultimate delusion, a precooked TV dinner with compartments full of impossibilities like "forever" and "completeness" and "ultimate fulfillment," all of which give people permission to accept stasis, to step off the merry-go-round of constant metamorphosis. Frankly, the idea of spending my life with one person frightens me. I have seen people decide that the self found with their mate is the self they will remain—known, non-threatening, and undeniably safe—until death. I don't want to gel and harden.

Without sounding glib, so far the only safety I've managed to find has come from accepting the relentless inevitability of change. This could be just another coping mechanism, a strategy not so unlike marriage in that it tricks me into feeling that I, and not the cosmic universe, am in control, but my view of relationships is accordingly nomadic: I accept that people who feel, change. Feelings change, relationships to feelings change, desire changes. When I commit to a person, I commit to the experience we will have together; I commit to the process of growth that comes from building the trust underlying our intimacy, to working through differences and issues. I accept that the person I may have needed and adored five years or even five months ago, the person with whom I created an environment of stability and constancy, may not be the person I need and adore now, when I want a companion with whom I can experience myself in a way that feels vast and fluid.

Don't get me wrong: resisting the urge to succumb to that cozy space of the romantic fairy tale isn't easy. At the ripe old age of twenty-seven, I find myself reconsidering marriage and the idea of the sixty-year partnership. I am falling in love again and this time even I want to find some way to dull the nagging fear of its demise, of that terrible, seemingly inevitable leave-taking. Suddenly marriage lurks in the wanderings of my mind, seducing me with its abstraction, its promise to thwart or somehow fool death, to let me live in this love forever. Because even though I have learned to live with change and to see each new lover as a divine gift, I still am not immune to the hideous pain of letting go. But making a friend of this pain and learning how to live with the discomfort of transition seems, right now at least, to be a worthwhile struggle and the ultimate commitment: a rite of passage on my life's path.

Homeward Bound

My SINGLE friends are searching for true love. They are starting to worry. The talent pool is dwindling. I try to be encouraging and offer helpful advice. What I always say is this: "Start mashing the panic button immediately."

I explain that, biologically speaking, finding a mate at this point would be a statistical anomaly, a freak of nature, a development so unlikely that it could be featured in the *Weekly World News* alongside the baby that is half-human and half-alligator. As a friend, I can do no less.

I have to dispense this advice because I am a role model and a pillar of the community. Not only am I married to a lovely, intelligent woman, but I have three adorable daughters. I own a home; I'm gainfully employed; and the goiter is successfully being treated by medication. The only thing I could possibly complain about is that having daughters is not quite the same thing as having, you know, heirs. Three times my wife had a chance to pony up a son, and three times she failed. This creates a huge problem in terms of estate planning. There are moments when, deep amid diapers and baby food, it occurs to me that I've gone to all this trouble for nothing.

But enough about me. Let's talk about my single friends, who spend their lives flitting from party to party, hitting happy hours after work, sailing on the weekends, jetting to Europe, screwing on the beach with beautiful strangers, sleeping late on Sunday mornings, power brunching and reading Victorian novels by the armload. Obviously, these pathetic individuals need to get married and have kids as soon as possible. Their pain is enormous.

Consider the case of a friend I will call Lucas. Lucas is a professionally successful man with lots of money and unlimited freedom. Lucas is now ready to transfer some of that success to the personal realm. Lucas talks like this:

"I've been reviewing my situation, going over my professional and personal portfolio as it were, and I think I'm ready to take the next step, settle down, start a family."

I try to point out to Lucas that, as he envisions his master plan, there seems to be only the most tangential, indeed a barely inferred, involvement of another live human being. To make his plan work, he will need to include, possibly even as a full partner, another person, someone who is very possibly a woman.

"Right. And that spells trouble," he says gravely.

Women have the same problem. Regardless of one's
sex, a mate is not a consumer item. To buy a new car, you
just need to compare prices and take some test-drives;
but when it comes to finding a human partner, you need
an entire mating strategy, and, frankly, it must incorporate risk, the surrender of control over one's destiny. At
the altar, the minister should say, "Do you take this man
to be your lawfully wedded husband, even though that
might prove to be hideously stupid?"

But no minister will say that, because marriage is sold
as an extension of true love. People shroud themselves in
true love as though it will excuse them from a rational
analysis of the situation. True love means you don't only
love someone but are "in love" with the person, a state
of being that transcends the will, that is not purposeful
or intentional but rather an immutable fact of life, a
condition. The difference between loving someone and
being in love is the same as the difference between
kneeling on the ground and being a midget.

I advise my friends: Beware of love. You want a mate,
not an object of adoration. If your decision to get married is contingent upon being in love, you run the risk
of conjoining with someone whose deep inner mon-
strousness has been obscured by your blind infatuation.
You should never get hitched simply because you are in
some kind of emotionally aroused state that is surely going to peter out in a year or two.

Love begins as a sonnet, but it eventually turns into a
grocery list. Therefore you need someone with whom
you can go to the supermarket.

So perhaps I am not what you would call an incurable romantic. But you have to understand the central fact of love: It is a bait-and-switch operation. You are genetically compelled to fall in love with someone who is beautiful or handsome, sweet, charming, funny, who acts as though you are the center of the universe, who crawls into your bed and sets you to panting. You undergo a mind meld. Suddenly, you anticipate each other's sentences; you get each other's jokes before anyone else in the room; you agree on Tiepolo, Trollope, Dilbert. The joy of this coming together is such that you seek a societal and familial sanction for it, and thus go through a ritual known as holy matrimony. Soon there is a new entity in the relationship: a fetus. The genes encoding your susceptibility to the love toxin have been perfectly replicated in the offspring, who will burst, violently, from the womb of the mother, radically changing the very environment in which the genetic replication became possible. The love partners must now devote all their psychic energies to raising a squealing, helpless, diapered individual, who gradually turns into a brat and then a teenager and then grows up to fall in love and repeat the cycle.

Not that marriage is bad! But by design a marriage—a mating—must change. The big things you thought were so important, like a shared aesthetic, like all that intellectual compatibility, decline in significance. The relationship becomes a series of little things. On little things does a marriage rise and fall.

My wife and I realized we were meant for each other

when we discovered our mutual interest in drinking coffee and reading the newspaper at a leisurely pace. We no longer do anything at a leisurely pace, but to this day we have a ritual in which I wake her up by bringing her a cup of joe. I would say that's 35 percent of our bond right there. Recently, I put some flavored beans— French vanilla—into the mix, and she was so revolted I thought she might call a lawyer.

Repeat after me: The little things count.

With three kids, we don't have time to mind meld. We see about one movie a year together. We sometimes go out to dinner and talk, and that's a blast, because we make lists of things that we like about our life, trying to remember how and why we got into this mess, and we plan fantastic, improbable trips, usually child-free, where we imagine recapturing the ol' mind meld (and screwing on the beach!). But on a typical day, we have no conversations whatsoever, just one or two "information transfers." For the sake of efficiency, it is essential that neither party gums up the transfer with irrelevant details about, for example, some story I'm working on or her book project (I think it has something to do with JFK).

Daily, one delights in the little things. Like my wife's nose. God, what a nose she has! Her nose is the gift that keeps on giving. It brings to mind a fine wind instrument, a delicate combination of straight lines and curves, upturned at the end but not impishly so, the nostrils flared intriguingly, the whole assemblage strikingly aristocratic, in stark contrast to my own thuggish, misshapen, Neanderthal protuberance. I think years ago my nose somehow detected her nose and issued a mating cry, envisioning our bond as a kind of gene therapy.

Counterbalancing the nose is Mary's extremely unfortunate tendency to take heroically long showers. For her a shower is as elaborate as triple-bypass surgery. Often she says to me, on a Saturday morning, in a tremulous voice, "Can I take a shower now?" and I say "No!" —outraged by the suggestion, knowing it will pretty much ruin the whole morning. She inevitably pleads her case and prevails, and something like an hour and a half later, having performed her various mysterious girlie hair rituals, she descends the staircase, cover-girl perfect. I solemnly declare, "Our long national nightmare is over."

Every marriage has its dark days. When a married friend tells me he's having a rough time, I try to perk him up with a biology analogy.

"It could be worse," I say. "There are male honeybees whose genitals literally explode during copulation. This plugs up the queen and prevents any other males from impregnating her."

"Exploding genitals? Is that fatal?"

"Extremely."

Bill Cosby said recently that it's not hard to be married for thirty-three years. You just go home at night. Perhaps there were times when Cos didn't quite make it home. But he got the formula right. You go home. You find little things to cherish. You have a favorite chair. You develop a coffee ritual, a storybook ritual, some running jokes. From little things emerges something big, and you realize that being married with kids is the essential condition of your life, an immutable fact, something you don't ever want to change.

Just like true love.

Adultery

I HAVE BEEN interested in adultery since 1967, when I discovered that my husband was having an affair. At first, it nearly ended our marriage. In time, though, I understood that my husband's infidelity had saved it. It told me that our marriage required changing if it was to become a vital union. And that I had to change, too.

I had been an independent, autonomous sexual rebel when we met. But I buried my spirited self and became staid and settled after we married. More interested in pot roast than passion. Someone other than the spitfire who had attracted him.

The woman I lost was the woman he wanted. Though it seemed he was unfaithful, paradoxically, he *was* faithful. To the spirit of the woman he married, to the kind of union he had imagined.

Our story has a happy ending. I reclaimed my lost self.

Called everyone I knew and told them he was fucking around. Told him that if he decided to leave, he'd have to take our infant son with him. Which made him stick around for a while.

I went back to graduate school, cultivated my own group of friends, followed my passions, traveled without my husband, became a writer. Made changes in myself and our relationship that his adultery indicated were required.

My experience told me I needed to think about adultery differently. Until then, I believed that having sex with someone other than your lawful partner necessarily ruins a marriage. But this wasn't true in mine. However hard it was, my marriage—and I—were better off because of it.

Adultery shatters the illusion of safety and predictability that generally comes when we're in a committed relationship. And this troubles most people. It troubled me. It forced me to realize that thinking myself a part of a couple was illusive, that each of us really exists in the world alone. These insights, though, are necessary to forge a mature working partnership rather than an infantile romanticized union.

I realized I needed a secure-enough relationship within which to do my work, to raise our children well, but one in which I retained my right to privacy, solitude, independence, and autonomy. Rather than demand an uncompromising fidelity to me, I tried to understand what I genuinely required from my husband, and to discover what he required from me. What I required, I dis-

covered, was fidelity (and not sexual fidelity) to our
working partnership, and not to one another.

What this means, of course, changes constantly and
it requires ongoing communication—arguments, com-
promises, and resolutions. It requires that we think
about what actions and attitudes are required of us if we
are to be genuinely faithful to our working partnership.
Ours is a noisy marriage and it makes many people nervous. It is far simpler, though, to me, less enriching, to
commit to a more traditional fidelity.

I BELIEVE THAT our culture requires us to think nega-
tively about adultery because it threatens the status quo.
It always involves risk, change, autonomy. As experience
showed me, any encounter with adultery forces us to
enter uncharted, and often unpredictable, emotional
terrain. We become someone other than the person
we've been.

Because adultery is the enemy of the predictable, settled life, but the ally of change, I believe there are valu-
able lessons in honoring its impulse, though we may
choose not to act upon it.

What, for example, is this impulse to be unfaithful
telling us that we need to know?

Once, when I was writing a novel about adultery, I
interviewed a score of married people having affairs. A
man, who longed to travel alone, had a lover who lived
three hours away. A woman, who wanted to become a
famous biographer, became the lover of the world's

foremost authority on her subject. Another woman yearned to be a painter; her lover was a street musician.

Without realizing it, these people had found themselves lovers who embodied their unfulfilled dreams. Though they believed that their adulteries were giving them something their marriages couldn't, I believed they replaced more significant change. It was less transgressive to their idea of who they should be in their marriages to, say, travel long distances to see a lover than to journey someplace alone, to sleep with someone important than to try to become important, to spend stolen hours with a musician than to use the time to create.

Their lovers uncannily revealed the secret yearnings of their hearts, the unrealized longings of their souls that requested fulfillment, but that were still thwarted.

I HAVE COME to see the impulse toward adultery as the self's yearning to realize its latent potential. Perhaps if we honor our frustrated desires, we will not need to stray.

Monogamy and Its Perils

W HEN YOU get married," an adult male friend told me when I was a teenager, "don't think about it. Don't think about being married. Just go through it day by day. If you think about it, you won't want to stay married." There was not, as I remember, a single successful marriage among any of my relatives during the years I lived with them. Perhaps they thought about the matter too much.

When I did marry I told this friend, a few days after the ceremony, that I wanted to be a very good husband, the best husband possible. He smiled. "Remember this: don't let your wife know your business," he said. "And you'll never be as good as you think you will be. You'll be as good as what you can live with." And, I suppose, as good as what she can live with as well.

Six years later, when I stood before my wife as the unfaithful husband, in something of the manner of a condemned prisoner, I realized that at that moment she hated me with as much sheer ferocity as she had probably hated anyone in her life.

There was, perversely, an ego affirmation in this, if only because it takes some degree of notice, even significance, to be worthy of hatred. But her loathing was more troubling than affirming: This was what I had always dreaded our relationship would amount to, in the end. Not the gradual, measured devotion of long-lasting love, nor the numbing if habitable drift of indifference, but rather the eruption of an eternal form of contempt, as old as the sexes themselves. This is a truth about marriage: So much of it seems so old, so long-ago lived, but each person in it is keeping strict accounts with a relentless memory. Nobody ever forgets a single moment of embarrassment, and nobody ever forgives a single moment of cruelty.

"I really thought you were different," she said scornfully. "But you're just like all men. You just think about yourself." This attack—completely justified in her eyes, as she felt that I had utterly betrayed her and through this betrayal had subjugated her to the prison of dutiful wifehood—was both wounding and amusing. It was wounding, of course, to be so bitterly denounced by someone whose respect and admiration meant everything to me. And it was amusing to be linked with this subspecies called men after several years of generously bestowed exceptionalism.

I should not have been amused. I had heard my mother and sisters talk about the worthlessness of men, of black men particularly. There is a certain special dilemma in monogamous marriage for black men and women that I was not fully cognizant of when we got married six years before. There is an entire history of bitterness and betrayal, from slavery onwards, that both black men and black women must bear, each having, at some critical moment, absolutely failed the other. During slavery, black marriage was never recognized as a truly sacred institution, and after slavery an air of recrimination existed between black men and black women: The men accused the women of being sellouts, of sleeping with white men, loving a white Jesus, and complaining of the failures and cowardice of black men. In return, the women said that the men were weak, that they cringed before white men, and treated their women violently only because they did not have the nerve to face the real source of their frustration; they contended that, secretly, the men desired white women, the sexual conquest of whom would serve as the political fulfillment of their manhood. Growing up as a fatherless black boy, I felt the weight of this mistrust. No one yearned more than I to fulfill the duties of being father and husband; to show the world—both black and white—that I, as a black man, was not the moral failure so many supposed me to be; to be the father that I deserved as a son and the husband that my mother deserved as a wife. I wanted my marriage to be a statement, clarion-clear, that it was possible in this world that a black person could make another truly happy and would truly want to.

Be forewarned: This essay was not meant to be a confession of an adulterous encounter, the moment of crisis in my marriage and how it survived. In this era of the tabloid, I find confession to be cheaply wrought and trite. If I am drawn to such a confession, it is only as an antidote for my recent memoir, *Daughters: On Family and Fatherhood*, where I appear, despite my shortcomings, as the loving husband and father. By describing myself as true and loyal to a black wife and black children, by portraying myself as a black Ward Cleaver, I made myself into the man I imagined myself to be— and into something far more wonderful than I actually was.

So to confess a brief bout of clumsy, obsessive adultery, as destructive as it was puerile, yet as richly instructive, in its way, as any sin, stands as something of a counter-narrative ego to my *Daughters* persona, a kind of thumbing of my nose at the rewards for all of my good works. Do I have to be good, in some bourgeois sense, because I am a black man? Or, as a bourgeois black man, do I have to stand as a counter-narrative to all the black rogues of the world?

When I was a boy, there was a man in my neighborhood whose face had been horribly disfigured by his girlfriend after she caught him with another woman. She poured together a concoction of lye and Coca-Cola and threw it on him. Neighbors say that you could hear her rapid-fire curses and his bloodcurdling screams, intermingling like two supremely anguished arias, for at least a city block. She went to jail. He went mad. She never returned to the neighborhood, and he walked the streets ever after, as familiar as the mailman, as pitied as a mangled dog, as dreaded as the horror he had become, always drunk, his ruined face, open and unhealed for all to see, always asking for a cigarette.

For many months after that incident, I was terrified by women. I thought it wise not to do anything to any of them that might make them do that to me. "Boy, you don't be having no woman control your life. That man," a patron in a barbershop once said to me, referring to our maimed neighbor, "is living testimony of what it costs a man not to be pussy-whipped by no woman out here. A woman try some shit like that on me, I'm goin' stick my foot so far up her goddamn ass that it won't even be funny." My mother used to tell my sisters, "Don't let no man out here mistreat you. But if he do, remember he got to sleep sometime. And you make sure to take care of that nigger's ass when he do."

I TURNED TO my wife at the moment when my marriage seemed to be dissolving with the hope that she might, as I assumed she wished very much to do, slap my face with great violence. In the theater of marriage, such moments of operatic excess can be good: The partners in such close and closed confines need opportunities to "act out."

But the moment passed between me and my wife. Her hatred subsided. She never struck me. Indeed, almost immediately, she took the wifely high road and chose to pity me instead. Implicit in her reaction was not only forgiveness but also a certain acknowledgment, required on my part, fully understood on her part, that she was the morally superior partner. But this was only the short-term response. In the long term my wife responded elegantly and gracefully: She set her sense of superiority aside. If a monogamous marriage—whether black or white—is to endure, any partner's failure must be a shared burden. She learned to live with her disappointment, and even to learn from it, as I learned to live with my shame.

And so we learned to live with each other anew—and probably better, for it all. It is a poignant and painful point to remember that marriage requires taking one for better or for worse. After all, everyone is wounded in the same old places, and there are limits to what can be achieved by picking at the scabs of one another's faults. We hardly need the sensational example of O. J. and Nicole Brown Simpson to understand that monogamous marriage can be a barbarous institution. James McMichael's recent account of the breakup of his second marriage, *Each in a Place Apart*, or Marvin Gaye's 1978 album, *Here, My Dear*, about the breakup of his first marriage—these works remind us that nothing brings out the explosive anger that lies beneath the surface of the relations between men and women like the moment when a marriage is no longer tenable, when one thinks of how much one has endured for the other's sake. Marriage at the point of its dissolution becomes something that one most terrifyingly wishes to hold on to because it is, alas, better than nothing, or better with this person than with the possible persons one might meet or might have met. It is perhaps the sheer accident of it all, winding up with this person instead of some other, that overwhelms at times. Marriage, in its barbarous civility, in its impossible dependence and impossible expectation, assures one that in the vast meaninglessness of the world, one can, only through the most monumental and absurd of accidental unions, hope to find the true rudder of meaning, at last.

This Is My Last Affair

WHEN YOU'RE single, it doesn't really occur to you, "Hey, I think what I really need is a hopeless, all-consuming affair with a married woman." But once an affair begins, you can't really imagine what your life was like before it. In the passion of the moment, one of the first things to go is your perspective.

Let me call her A. For a year and a half, we had what can only be called a "torrid" affair. I am single and live in the city; A. is a stay-at-home mom who lives in those suburbs over the bridge, through the tunnel and around the mountain. To say of A. that she is a suburban house-wife is to do her an injustice. During our affair, she was the most electric of humans, a live wire, burning hot. For better or worse, I hope we've all felt this way about someone at one time.

I met A. through an adult education class—we'd

flirted, rather shamelessly I'm afraid, the entire time. After the last class, A. took me on a moonlit, wind-rushed
ride in her Miata convertible. Within a week, we were
in the obsession zone: hushed phone calls, clandestine
meetings, hotel rooms, anonymous post-office boxes,
even a remote control that granted me access to the priv-
ileged world of her (and her husband's) gated community.

My love for A. felt real at the time, but the affair took
on a life of its own. It was as if we were writing a really
terrific novel, but one that no one else would ever read.
We were, in effect, completely swayed by our own fic-
tions. Everything around us seemed erotic and dangerous. And, drunk with intrigue and lust, we promised
each other the world.

THE TELEPHONE rests on a bookshelf next to my
desk, lifeless plastic and wires. It was one of the first gifts
she gave me, and for a year and a half it appeared as vola-
tile and menacing as a handgun. I'd wait for it to explode. And when it did ring, I'd leap for it like a Secret
Service agent in action. I'd pick up, never knowing
whether she'd say, "Come see me right now," or, "It's
all over."

Several friends have since confided that they stopped
calling when I was likely to answer; they could not bear
the disappointment in my voice. "Hello?" I'd ask hope-
fully. When I recognized that it was *not her*, my tired ex-
hale would betray me: "Oh, it's just you." By the end of
the affair, I owed a mountain of apologies.

But I was clueless, and there were so many phone calls to await, to plan and plot and pine for. There was her home phone, her car phone (so many risky possibilities there!) and numerous pay phones. I even used to call her at the pool, where she swam alone at night, until one evening, a little tipsy, I dialed a number and she hung up right away. I'd actually called her at home by mistake, where she was in bed reading with her husband, and I had to wait twelve agonizing hours before I could call again and apologize.

Deep into the affair, I would call at dinner, knowing he would be there—one ring, just to let her know. On Christmas Eve, she called from the upstairs bathroom to tell me that she loved me, while her kids hung their stockings with care. When you're the other man, you get off on the danger; even worse, you mistake it for love.

Sometimes the danger felt palpable. One night, while digging through my freezer, I found a perfectly placed book of matches in a half-eaten pint of ice cream and became convinced that *he* had been in my house and was sending me a message. That night I slept with a chair in front of the door and dreamed of Komodo dragons loosed upon me. The next morning, when I called A., she told me that she doubted her husband had put the matches there—he wasn't clever enough.

Several months into the affair, A. bought a brand-new Jeep Grand Cherokee Laredo, a purchase that came out of the blue and seemed to send an ominous message: She would be staying in the big house behind the gate.

I began to keep track of all similar vehicles. Do you

know how many brand-new Jeep Grand Cherokee Laredos there are? Where I live, they are apparently giving
them away. I quickly learned to recognize their silhou-
ette, as spotters had picked out enemy planes during
World War II. This was a hugely demanding task, but I
knew any one of them *might be her.*

The world became nothing *but* her. The mailbox; my
car, where she might leave a note; a certain parking ga-
rage, where we'd once made love in the stairwell; the
view of her mountain from one of the city's hills; any
woman with great legs; all children; the bar she knew
I frequented; even, at times, something as big as the
moon, simply because we both stood under it.

Even the merely foolish began to seem romantic. After sneaking out of A.'s window at six in the morning,
her husband away on business (take heed, ye frequent
fliers!), the kids watching their first *Barney* of the day, I
would stop at the nearby gas station for espresso and a
scone and laugh at the stockbrokers fueling their Lexi
for the drive into the city. As if I were sleeping with all
their wives.

I would keep her lipstick-stained Champagne flutes
near my bed, and I once kept a bag of ice from her drink
in the freezer. I would drive an hour to share a cigarette
outside the grocery store. I spent thousands of dollars on
phone bills, hotel rooms, and a rather misbegotten week
in New York. I'm still paying for it. All of it.

WHEN YOU'RE in the throes of an affair, these are
some of the things you think about while lying in bed:

divorce and the decline of civilization, martinis, gun-shots. Then, in the next three seconds, another herd of ominous beasts tramples across the vast open plain of your mind: Are there others? Is her husband as big a jerk as he seems? How will you get along with the kids? But you still can't fall asleep. You read but retain nothing. Lights on, lights off. The drone of your brain. When you eventually do fall asleep in the Fitzgerald-dark night, the front grilles of Jeep Grand Cherokee Laredos fly at you en masse, like shimmering bats.

The good stuff? Oh, there's plenty of that. Every great song in the world being about and for you. The high rush of a hotel afternoon. Being kissed nearly to death in downtown alleys. Shopping for lots of new lingerie. The thrill of secrets. But these things, you realize finally and with some gratitude, cannot and do not last. Love, real love, you begin to pray, outlives the moment.

When the affair is over, this last lesson comes home to roost. What do you have? A cardboard box filled with letters and small gifts (gifts you once thought charming but that now seem so pallid), some tawdry photographs you wouldn't show a soul and a lot of regrets, because you know that damage has been done—to everyone involved—and realize that what had almost killed you was not love at all.

THE LAST dregs of our affair wound down slowly, pathetically, from sheer fatigue. She *had* decided to stay in the big house, and over the course of a few months the visits and the phone calls became less frequent, then simply stopped. Neither of us ever said it was over; it just was. Sometime last spring, ensconced in my small apartment, I began to see that the world was bigger than me and my trials.

At the same time, a good friend of mine got involved in a similar affair. I could see in Chris's face not only how silly I had become but how ordinary my affair with A. had been. My pat answer to friends' concerns had always been, "This is different; this is the real thing." But it wasn't, it was the same old thing, as old as the hills.

When I run into him at our local pub, Chris has what I call the "piranha look." He's a man who's up to his neck in the Amazon with a school of piranhas tearing at his flesh, and he's telling you how absolutely happy he is, how great B. is.

I saw him again last night. When I walked into the bar, Chris said nothing; he simply pushed a piece of paper in my face and commanded me to read it. It was a letter he had written to *her*, and he wanted to make sure that each phrase was correct, all the nuances expressed, each comma in place. He truly believed that if this one letter were written perfectly, she would leave her husband.

I talked to Chris as best I could. It's not that he wouldn't listen to reason; he couldn't. I vowed right then and there to go home and write a few apologetic notes to nearly lost friends, then to pray for Chris, for his peace. Either that or go back to the bar and shoot him— for his own good.

Strange Perfume

IT PAINS ME in retrospect that I didn't give her more
fun and a better time. We were married for a quarter of
a century, and she died the same year, 1993, that our
divorce went through. Although from opposite back-
grounds, we were both by temperament conservators,
which gave us something in common and lent us an ex-
tra stability. That, with the illuminating presence of our
child, helped us last. Adultery, which by definition is
embedded in marriage and is not like a bachelor screwing around, may have, too, unless you assume we would
have been better off wedded to other spouses, which
oddly enough I'm not quite prepared to do.

I was born into the Protestant establishment in 1932,
my father a lawyer for Davis Polk & Wardwell, a white-
shoe Wall Street firm, and was christened at J. P. Mor-
gan's old church, St. George's, on Stuyvesant Square.

But I was sharply and rebelliously disillusioned by my inside look—the Greenwich, Connecticut, cotillions where Lester Lanin, the society bandleader, himself used to ask me if I had forgotten how to smile; the anti-Semitic country clubs, yacht clubs, and Fifth Avenue clubs my parents belonged to—and ended up pretty much disinherited by my father when he died. Instead, at Harvard I enlisted in the retrograde mold represented by John Dos Passos, John Reed, or Henry Thoreau, going off and rooting my first novel out of the experience of working for five months in the Ringling Bros. Circus, then insisting upon being drafted into the U.S. Army in 1955 in spite of serious asthma and a horrendous stutter, when many of my classmates were obtaining grad-school deferments. Later I lived on the Lower East Side while writing a novel about New York boxing and another one about the Brownian motion of life in a welfare hotel.

Probably because of the vise of my stutter I was a little late in losing my virginity (twenty-three), but in due course married an attractive, idealistic woman, a UN statistician and Bennington graduate—a union that dissolved amicably after four years, with much travel (Sicily, British Columbia) but neither the glory of children nor the specter of infidelity. This was a divorce that came too easily, in the no-fault mode—even our lawyers were partners. It lacked a moral dimension, and I dreamed of her in poignant scenarios for years afterward. Despite my bohemian proclivities, I acquired a distaste for the idea of divorce ever after. Better a folie à deux, stressed and buffeted by time, sociology, and psyche, as my second marriage may have been, than such a bland exit.

In 1968 I remarried. This woman, Marion Magid, was an editor at *Commentary* magazine, a Barnard graduate, thirty-six, dramatically witty, formidably well read, a master of conversational innuendo but never cruel, a high-octane interpreter of what was wrong with Tennessee Williams for *Commentary* and what was hip in London and Amsterdam for *Esquire.* Raised in the Bronx, she had known Yiddish before English and had translated Isaac Bashevis Singer's famous short story "Yentl the Yeshiva Boy" (later a Barbra Streisand movie; Marion quit translating for him only because he groped her). She acted a bit in the Yiddish theater, her name once in lights on a Broadway marquee, and had written two scripts that the avant-garde photographer Robert Frank made films out of. She'd also written and edited for the Zionist literary magazine *Midstream;* had worked for a TV producer at ABC and at Cleveland Amory's *Celebrity Register* and for a New York psychoanalyst, too, for several years.

Marion was compelling, handsome, with a wonderful "whiskey voice" with which to launch her bons mots, good legs, a wide, generous mouth, and shoulder-length reddish-brown hair of the coarse, pleasing texture of a fox's pelt. When dressed for success, which was not ordinarily her habit, she wore short leather skirts, net stockings, and what she called "Krafft-Ebing" fantasy boots, in those salad days. A woman of parts, and I was now marrying into the Jewish establishment; New York's chief judge of the court of appeals performed the ceremony. Though I was not her first WASP nor she my first Russian Jew, we were amused by the contrast when she rattled off the names of her previous admirers: Klaus, Gert, Werner, Baruch, Maier. She hadn't been married before because the love of her life had recently married an Israeli girl, and, like me, Marion was at loose ends. Her mother, meeting me with alarm, confided to her that my Ivy League teeth looked too good to be true, must be bridgework. My mother sailed to Europe the day before our wedding.

Marion and I met at an Upper West Side party, and I called *Commentary*, at the offices of the American Jewish Committee, the next day so we could finger the appeal of our exoticism again. My fragility had not put her off, and I sensed in her a kindred odd duck. Her poli-sci, Nietzsche specialist had recently married the Israeli woman, and Marion was suffering bad bouts of depression, getting by on deli takeouts and already plagued by the writer's block that would become her chief grief for the rest of her life. Postcards from Edmund Wilson could carry you only so far, like the kudos I, on my side, had won. I was more manic, a trifler with tigers and elephants at Ringling Bros. and later in India, as well as with death in its Arctic and later Antarctic guise. I was in a fertile phase, finishing maybe my best book, *Notes from the Century Before*, interviews with frontiersmen, and was living in a new apartment in Greenwich Village that was a good deal less bleak than her digs on Thirty-fourth

Street. We needed as well as amused each other and, more important, quickly recognized a rare and basic affinity: that we were each professional conservators. My work consisted of going out on long forays to try to reconstruct the reality of the frontier by talking to old men in shacks alongside great virginal rivers, about old-growth forests and bears and ice. She at her magazine and in the cafés of upper Broadway, because of her elegant, deep-water knowledge of Yiddish, was besieged by lonely, audienceless poets, memoirists, and fiction writers whose only market was the *Jewish Daily Forward*. Our heartstrings were thus tied in parallel fashion to doomed but historic enterprises that remarkably few people cared to pay any attention to in that winter of 1967–1968. Though ignorant of Yiddish, I'd spent hundreds of hours in the same cafeterias, knew countermen with numbers tattooed on their arms, and had lived for two and a half years in Europe without ever setting foot on German soil in reaction to this. Marion, by contrast, had gone directly to Berlin in the mid-1950s on a Fulbright fellowship to study Bertolt Brecht, thereby outraging her immigrant father—that she'd go to Germany so soon after the Holocaust and indeed would even aspire to be an actress—much as my own contrarian acts and wanting to be a novelist had angered my father from the opposite side.

Both complex, feisty souls who lived by our nerves, we had tried to set our own course in life, and after two or three dates she asked, "Do you ever sleep over?" She had funny tales of other artist/intellectuals who would carefully study the books on her shelves instead of making a pass and then try to put her down for authors she didn't have, while mainly of course whining because their own books weren't there. She had not expected to experience motherhood but to burn with a hard, bright thinker's light instead. Yet by and by her pregnancy energized us to marry, as we might have been too dithery to do otherwise. I'd had to be prompted to marry the first time also, this passivity in my relations with women presumably being a legacy from my complicated mother, who I like to say gave me "the fright of my life," as Marion, who knew her, agreed. Suffice it to say, no woman who wears fishnet stockings, short leather skirts, and black leather boots should object if her suitor likes to play the gawky, dominated boy in lovemaking. The skit just gradually came to seem inappropriate to us after we'd got married and had a baby on the way, and she confessed anyhow that her own kinkiness consisted in not being able to make love as freely with somebody she loved as with people who didn't matter—if she loved them her libido shut off.

In the gaiety of being married and seeing my child born, then being up with the baby twice a night and scribbling ideas, the knack I had fashioned in my travel book for speaking to a reader had turned into my first essays. I was scarcely aware of how this happened, but I poured it on, a bookful in just two years—the baby inevitably inventing herself too as we went along.

Yet, REACHING FORTY without ever having broken a marital vow and quite a rara avis in uptown or downtown circles for that, I was restive. Marion used to joke that men ought to have two wives, one for company, one for sex, and she knew virtually no man of mature years who had been sexually faithful. We'd loaned our apartment, in fact, to one of her closest buddies for his assignations. Another went around town showing off nude photos of his ex-wife "to get her married again." But she said what distinguished a tacky man from a decent man was whether he exempted his wife from the messy experience of hearing at secondhand that he'd seduced her best friend. Or in another context, powerful editors in the magazine world divided the ingenues they had access to between those they slept with and those they brought home to their parties. It seemed a time of "general copulation," in the phrase from Peter Weiss's exemplary play *Marat/Sade*.

Marion had never had an orgasm and believed herself not good at sex, though I tended to blame myself because I'd never given my first wife an orgasm either—at least not till after we'd split up and she came back to visit me and taught me how the Frenchman and the Hungarian whom she was seeing at the UN did it. And it had required the patient yet peremptory tutoring of a couple of women whom I knew between my marriages to further rid me of the boyish selfishness that had marked my sexuality until I was past thirty. Absorbed nowadays in a different phase of life, helping to find a clever pediatrician, a lively nursery school, moving with Marion and our daughter to a larger apartment, I was less selfish as a person but more tired or perfunctory as a sexual partner.

At *Commentary* parties the mood turned tenser, however, as politics, not literary gossip, became the focus around the time of the 1968 teachers' strike in Brooklyn, when black community boards squared off against Jewish administrators. Neoconservatism was an embryo at these soirees, and an Israeli visitor might stand up before our seated group and describe with visible relish how abjectly a Palestinian prisoner would break under the beatings administered off-street in a police van. Vietnam was an additional issue. Marion and I had our first fights over the invasion of Cambodia by American troops, because, for her, toughness in Southeast Asia seemed to translate into future support for Israel in the Middle East. The old things whose survival engrossed me—wetlands, wildernesses to be preserved—had no cost to America even if you didn't care about them as a cause, whereas I began to think that neoconservatism, as spearheaded by *Commentary* in championing the South Vietnamese regime, the Argentinian junta, the Salvadoran dictatorship, was warping our foreign policy away from a Jeffersonian involvement with the Third World, and that her interest had shifted from Isaac Bashevis Singer to Menachem Begin and Yitzhak Shamir.

From this point on, we felt an undertow in our marriage, and I suggested, not joking, that we move to New Mexico. So many friendships were breaking up over politics in this neocon versus liberal little world that our situation differed only in being marital, and I was determined that the gravity of divorce not evolve out of disagreements over the evening news. What happened to us in particular, however, was that Marion's first love, the Nietzschean poli-sci professor whom she had fallen for way back in Berlin in the 1950s, lost his young wife to cancer; and this—as he began telephoning daily for solace, a man with heart problems but a roly-poly, untidy vigor, a wispy spade beard and playful irony—together with other callers, bachelors who were dependent on her in Toronto, San Francisco, and elsewhere for company at night on the phone, doubled the strain. It seemed to me a platonic promiscuity, but since I was out prowling bars two or three evenings a week, after picking up our daughter at school and taking care of her during the afternoon, I can't say whose loneliness had precedence. We still sometimes had happy weekends, when she might bring home the desperate half-English, half-Yiddish manuscript of a frantic refugee wetly escaped from the Soviet Union, who had showed up in her office holding the hollowed-out hairbrush in which he'd concealed the microfilm of his gulag memoirs. Lavishing her free time, she would somehow transmute his anguish to publishable prose, and after it appeared in the magazine, the guy would win some kind of book contract or teaching post and be safely launched.

My twenty essays for *The Village Voice* had gotten me *Sports Illustrated* assignments in the South and trips abroad—to Cairo for *Harper's* and on to Cyprus, Jerusalem, later Khartoum, later San'a. We hadn't moved to New Mexico, though we did buy a cabin in northern Vermont. But it wasn't distant enough, and the five-year itch toward promiscuity, which I suspect is built into most men, was chafing me in any case. I bridled before the wall of the taboo against adultery, procrastinated, took refuge in my lack of confidence, dodging seductions and making the barriers inconvenient as well as explicit and thus tougher to scramble across. But at last, down in Texas, I fell in love. It was on a trip to write about red wolves, and Donald Barthelme had given me the number of a friend in his hometown of Houston who had kicked out her husband of umpteen years a few months before. We would meet in the towns of Winnie or Liberty, Texas, or in Cameron, Holly Beach, or Johnsons Bayou, across the state border in Louisiana, and drive the clamshell roads at night listening for wolf howls and admiring the nearly wild Brahman cattle silhouetted against the sunset or dawn, grayish-bluish humped animals that could survive the winds, mosquitoes, drought, heat, rains, and frost.

I hustled another assignment to go out with a number of Cajun trappers in their pirogues while they collected their night's worth of raccoons, mink, nutria, muskrats, otters; it gave me a horror of furs. I went to the annual rat-skinning contests and cross-dressing balls and crabmeat, crawfish, and jambalaya fests of southwest Louisiana, to pepper-sauce factories, egret and stork sanctuaries, and sometimes would show up at midnight at our agreed-upon motel with mud to my knees and eat shrimps, oysters, and chicken-fried steak with my friend. She had a job teaching art and two teenage sons and drove to these Gulf Coast beaches from her Texas-style patioed house. She was slim, lithe, small-faced, and frizzy-haired like my first wife, but less innocent, more socially and professionally ambitious, and her accent was of her birthplace, New Orleans, with hints of the French Caribbean behind that, the ultimate in sultriness for pillow talk. If I wasn't going to New Mexico, maybe I'd move here! My infatuation was so intense that at Houston's airport, going in or out, I groaned.

I wangled other assignments—went to Pilottown at the Mississippi's mouth to watch commercial garfishing and into the freshwater swamps upriver to eat squirrels with bobcat trappers, or visited plantation houses for *Travel & Leisure*, and went to Big Bend on the Rio Grande with a puma hunter. Her name would catch at my heart when I murmured it to myself back in New York, but what held me up was the daily delight of waking up in the same house as my daughter, not as an absentee father two thousand miles away, and the fact that I did love my wife to her dying day. And abruptly the momentum broke when my Houston friend's elder son told his father I was at the house and told his mother that his father was coming with a gun. It was no idle threat. We fled hastily to a motel and I returned to New York, alarmed that she should have been married for so long to somebody who, after their separation, would resort to a gun. It was southern enough but too southern for me, and indeed ten years later, when we met casually, she told me another man she was breaking up with had just threatened her with a gun. The passion of that tongue and that thrilling voice came with a price.

At some point around then, Marion went up to Cornell with our daughter to visit her Nietzschean widower, who was phoning every night with his Germanic Santa Claus voice, inserting himself as a kind of uncle in my daughter's affairs, to see whether Marion wanted to leave me for him. At least so I interpreted the trip. But she came back. I doubt whether she could face leaving the city, and she also said she didn't consider the jumbled household of her friend, with two motherless girls, would be an improvement for Molly upon life in our more focused home, with a decent school.

Like numerous marriages of the era, one could argue with equal cogency that adultery splintered ours or preserved it, enabled it to last or split it into pieces. Adultery, like "adult" books, has little relation to *adultus*, Latin for "grown," because it can be that still-nineteen-year-old sidling down the street, looking into lit windows for a woman alone. Yet it only occurs within the context of a marriage, and may not really be about sex—though I think nature in a schematic sense designed men for polygyny, once each successive child's period of toddlerhood is gone. Men have a sack of seeds to sow, and such a theory does not contradict the adolescent aspects of cheating on your wife because nature did not construct men with the expectation that they were going to live very long. My wife's telephonic polyandry, as I called it—half a dozen men counting on the intimacy of her wit to buoy their lives daily or two or three times a week at least—may have been built into her, too. We stuck together by attending school plays, and for wee-hours warmth, and book collecting, and to confront the bureaucracies that everywhere try to make existence as difficult as they can. Her relationship to her mother was exceptionally close—she would converse or cry out to her in her sleep—and that oddity, too, while at first an obstacle, may have become a balancing factor that helped our marriage last.

THE PHONE lines hummed; the streets were priapic; the restaurants seemed full of forlorn people whose spouses had recently left them. There was this feeling to the seventies as of a creaking, corniced avalanche in the making. In a deteriorating society conduct tends to be improvised, and the sexual license of the counter-culture, as well as Vietnam and Watergate, had wet the underpinnings of the country. Union members who might have sheared a hirsute hippie a decade before looked pretty hairy themselves; traditional loyalties of many sorts were eroding toward the greed-grab that was to follow. Lots of people were getting divorced or having an extramarital affair who didn't need to. A friend of mine, in separate years, found two men she loved dead of heart attacks in her apartment—waking up to discover their corpses on her bed or her couch—and asked me whether orgasms were all that important, that we, and especially men, should search so hard for variety. My fragility or brusqueness prevented me from sleeping with anybody I didn't genuinely like; and probably in order to cut the sin of infidelity in half, I didn't sleep with married women nor with undergraduate students nor with the loves of friends. I regretted the failure of my marriage and yet not many of the specifics of my conduct, just as I wouldn't have regretted writing a novel that ultimately failed.

While teaching a semester at the University of Iowa, I fell into another involvement with a conservator, a woman who headed a social agency that helped the local elderly find housing and shop for food. She had written her master's thesis on a nearby community of Amish farmers, whose Sunday services she used to take me to, and an earlier thesis on the Indians of the Kuskokwim River in interior Alaska. She was interested in old customs, old heroes and adventurers. She was a Texan— willowy yet statuesque, dramatic in gesture yet sympathetic to people who weren't. She lent a comfort and glamour to the Mississippi-midwestern milieu that had attracted me to Iowa City in the first place, and our lovemaking, which was amateur, blundery, and delightful, was like the high school sweetheart I'd never had. She, again, was my age, and an appropriate partner, but I was too New York-ish to uproot myself and she too bound to Iowa by temper and by her career to move.

I may have been a bit like Marion in the quirk she had warned me of early on: that damper that psychologically throttled lovemaking with a loved one. It may have reinforced our original attraction to each other, which was honest and in earnest and which continued at the country place I had acquired. My best writing there was probably done during the years when I was sexually faithful, the directness of a clear conscience matching the spring water. I would meet her sleeper at the Montpelier, Vermont, train station on weekends, when she liked to pretend we were in a Russian novel—"*You will find us very dull in the country, Sergei*"—mimicking a Tolstoyan accent. Her sense of humor redeemed the dullness of being housebound, because she didn't like going far from the house outdoors.

Marion continued her round of editorial lunches and generously painstaking editing of young writers to get their first short stories into print, but at night her retinue of polyandrous callers kept unbosoming themselves in her ear, though sometimes speaking unpleasantly to me if I was the one who picked up the phone. One guy might spin his rotary dial to produce a long-distance Bronx cheer of clicks. Another might mock the latest essay of mine that had appeared; my subjects were "derelicts or animals," he said. I did indeed keep riding tugboats through Kill Van Kull to Newark Bay, or going into the woods with bear scientists, while prowling off-hour haunts such as the Lion's Head bar, which I enjoyed for its tabloid newspapermen with a different take on life from mine, and where I found a buddy who became a friend.

To make love with a woman you must pay some attention to her: In this fin de millennium, that has become heterosexuality's saving grace. Otherwise, the proverbial war between the sexes nearly ensures that you will start scrapping. She will remember her callous ex-husband or oafish dad or the last chump who tried to manipulate her or just plain everyday feminist exhortations. In part we resent the opposite sex because of the helplessness with which we lay for years in some big person's arms, without having had the later satisfaction of growing up to replicate them; and thus the wholesale anonymity of bathhouse same-sex promiscuity that pervaded Greenwich Village would not have worked between men and women even in those years.

My friend was a photographer's model who was finding modeling hard going as she aged. I was hobbling around with a hernia and parathyroid problems and whatnot and was touched. Women who make their living with their bodies have always reminded me of athletes, such as the boxers I'd written a book about in the 1950s and the baseball players I'd admired in the 1940s, with the mortality question telescoped. Her black flare of hair was turning crisper, her figure thicker, and she discovered with alarm that she was descending from glossy pages to newsprint, from top-of-the-line airport magazines to bottom-shelf "skin rags." The brisk professional photographers who paid a decent wage and made a game of it were calling younger models—she showed me her portfolio to test my sexuality through my breathing—and she was left with the Brooklyn shutterbug clubs, where ten or twenty cheapskates got their kicks from ogling her for a few bucks in "dues." Or a solo operator would put aside his camera and try to corner and paw her, having hired her presence for an hour, then in "revenge" trade her phone number to a scary deviant who phoned at midnight to ask her measurements, discuss poses, and threaten and revile her. She did do poses for a comic-strip artist in dominatrix costumes that he supplied, but his wife watched, joking about it, and it was an excuse for ordering in lunch.

Frightened—because where would it end?—she liked men more than women, nevertheless, and understood that her livelihood was grounded in their vulnerabilities. What she wanted from me, apart from the bookish talk and chat about trips to Africa that she didn't get from her dinner dates, who were mostly businessmen or professional men, was the simple reversal. "Kiss the Queen. Kneel to the Queen," she'd whisper as I licked her and she came six or seven times, purging those humiliations of the camera for the time being. Nobody should ever enter her again, she promised herself, without first doing the same—while I, for my part, sought spellbound to climb headfirst into the primal womb in our deep-swimming, almost pelagic, sessions. Then she'd do Air Force exercises while I unwound by watching Johnny Carson.

Trotting home through the sweet, funky Village streets with the lights of New Jersey glistering on the wide Hudson at the end of our block, hinting of trips west or to other rivers that were the inspiration of so many writers I loved—Cather, Twain, Faulkner, Anderson—I felt I was sideslipping trouble like a quick coyote and doing the possible, assembling a doable life. But when I actually entered our cozy apartment, dodging into the bathroom to scrub myself in the shower, I felt guiltier than a rat—trying to figure out if the perfume was finally off, if the soap's scent would mask it, before sneaking into our bed and trying to lie on the far side so Marion wouldn't smell my body if she awoke. Unless, on the other hand, I heard her purring and blowing into the phone in the next room to one of her polyandrous crew. Then I didn't feel like a bad husband. She was "the darling of our hearts" (as the phrase came to be) to so many men, each half in love with her, that I was merely sad.

INFIDELITY can be a cliché like trying to flee death or sexual insecurity, or the more casual hoist-a-beer cheer that you only "go around" once. It may seem to alchemize lies into white lies by siphoning off the poisons that might otherwise lay low a marriage. I prefer to think ours didn't fit any truism but was unique. Would we have found monogamy in New Mexico if we had moved? Instead we stayed put and provided a stable framework for our daughter to go to school and for us to work hard for twenty years, turning out two or three hundred issues of her magazine and my own set of books of the period. We played our word games, read classy novelists, ate good meals, passed our doctors' exams, and shared a mostly comfortable bed.

If you teach college students, as I do, you see the results of pell-mell divorce and concupiscence—homes that have fractured into shards; kids whose parents are no more than a ready credit card, who have lost track of where their titular paterfamilias actually is; kids who are sleeping together not for sex but only for company. I've met the father of a student of mine at a New York party who didn't know what his son was majoring in. An honest-to-goodness sea change has occurred, and Generation X is a name they accept for themselves because almost every basic remains an uncertainty. The torque applied to marriages now is unprecedented: the speed of travel, of electronic stimulation, the cultural crosshatch, the diverse titillation and rudderless liberation, the no-fault method of reckoning everything. Jobs are changed like a suit of clothes. Adultery is not biblical, but "acting out." Nothing is binding or even binary, not sexuality or ethics.

What can happen—to choose a painful, down-to-earth example—is that, through the miracle of TV, you can see people dying as you sit in your living room. You can see children shot in the West Bank by Israeli soldiers for the crime of stone throwing, and remember meeting, on a visit to Israel with your wife, the man now responsible for the aggressive new policy of shooting more children—sharing a Shabbat dinner with his family, in fact.

The Intifada, when it burst out in Israel's Occupied Territories in 1987, was like the Tet Offensive in Vietnam. It proved the conquering power's assumptions were wrong. In my weeks in Israel and a hundred New York discussions, one of those assumptions, at least at the leadership level, had been that Palestinians weren't quite human beings. Their grief, pride, courage, and feeling for home weren't real, and reprisals could grind them down. For some of my acquaintances, Arabs were a kind of unsleeping preoccupation, equivalent to the worst bigotry I had ever seen in the WASP neighborhoods in the Northeast, where I had grown up, though with the distinction that the deeds of the Nazis were rung in to justify any oppressive measure visited upon the Arabs. I came to believe that the reason I'd hear Gandhi and Martin Luther King, Jr., spoken of so slightingly was because of an unease with the reality of how a King or a Gandhi would have fared in the Occupied Territories.

Marion, meeting friends of mine, expressed a corresponding disparagement of their intellectual integrity and the character of their books on nature or the Middle East. I was enduringly touched by the angry slump to her shoulders, her disappointment and irony when I would come home sneezing because my allergy to cat fur had been triggered (most single women keep a cat): "Have you caught cold?" But our alliance gradually tore, despite the empathy we felt for each other. I remember a specific moment when it registered on me that I was traveling with the wrong crowd. We were driving to the Upper East Side with a man who, with his deep tan and good car, had done pretty well, like so many of her friends, riding the neocon wave. We were passing the Martinique Hotel, a welfare dumping ground at Thirty-second Street whose haggard beggars this lunchtime had spilled over the curb at the stoplight. They weren't blacks on this particular day, so the crux was poverty, not race. They were Appalachian-looking

whites—bony, vitamin-starved, despairing kids of ten
or twelve with faces out of Walker Evans or Dorothea
Lange, the product of some social cataclysm in coal
country. This man's father, if I recall, had had a horse
and wagon hauling junk in Winnipeg fifty years ago, but
when these hungry-looking, country-looking children
asked for change for groceries at his window, he was ex-
asperated, rolling it up—that he hadn't clear sailing all
the way uptown. It was of a piece with the neocon idea
that the problem of homelessness was being exaggerated
by liberals, and I made up my mind that I had better cut
and run.

I WAS IN love with Alaska, and in Alaska, at this point
with a person who had shown up at 6:30 A.M. at my door
in Fairbanks, where I was teaching for a week. We'd
talked, and after a side trip I flew down to Juneau, where
she lived, and, wildly, we did more than talk. She was a
public health nurse who had been flying out alone to
half a dozen Tlingit villages on the islands of the Alex-
ander Archipelago on a schedule of troubleshooter visits
for total health care, from prenatal to easing old people
into a gentle grave. Like me, she loved hearing old lore
and pristine stories, loved seeing wildlife and sizing up
individuals who had rarely encountered a bureaucracy
or perhaps even piped-in electricity before. On a ferry-
boat we went visiting some of her clientele, now that
she was preparing to take up a new job in Anchorage di-
recting the nursing care for all the tuberculosis patients

in the state. Our curiosity, our enthusiasms, our sexual personalities jibed, though she was much younger and more radical politically than me. She was a woman of salient mercy, constantly fighting for the best she could get for her patients—doctor visits, medevac flights, operations, preventive measures. She was the kindest person I've ever known and as intrepid as any. Our sorties to Eskimo hamlets and trappers' cabins, traveling all over Alaska together checking on Athabascan or Inupiat people who had caught TB, would imbalance this essay if I put them in. We stood on the ice of the Yukon River in January and the Arctic Ocean in February, and flew in tiny ski planes, seated on the floor, clasping each other in tandem, to see how a child on the Koyukuk River or the Holitna River was doing. Crooked Creek, Sleetmute, Red Devil, Point Hope, Kotzebue, Tanana, Angoon: We saw them all. She left nursing and eventually became an anthropologist, working with other Indians, preferring the single life to do that.

Not surprisingly my marriage broke up by and by, though years after some of my friends had expected it to. ("We thought you liked being unhappy," one said.) Our daughter was at Harvard and heading for graduate school, but because it had been a full decade since more than a couple of my friends had been welcome visitors in our home, she knew almost none of them, only Marion's circle, an exclusion I'd come to resent. I felt quarantined, with Marion beginning to jeer generically at WASPS—distressed to the brink of wanting to jump out a window when I left.

I'd expected that my wife's first love would at last move in. But he didn't, and so it was I who shared with my daughter watchman's duty at Marion's deathbed in the hospital several years later. I was not an inappropriate presence, because I still cared for her and respected her as a brave partisan for what she believed in. I admired her passionate motherhood and her faithful affection for her many friends, and was present to the last, when the morphine the doctor had prescribed very peacefully suppressed, first her fierce, ebullient wit, and then her breathing, high over 168th Street of the city she loved.

My father would not have approved of our marriage because Marion was Jewish but would have disapproved of our getting divorced more. He once told me the only excuse for indulging even in infidelity was if you were married to a person who was mentally ill, without specifying whether my mother's spates of hysteria had made him do so. I've said she gave me the fright of my life but have never been able to define it through a series of incidents that connect like dots. In the warp and woof of our marriage my mother and Marion's father were heavy bettors, although both of them were spirits from a world eclipsed. Yet I think our failures and betrayals were mutual and common to our era, driven by our era, and that our stopgap solutions were improvised in a fervor of stubborn conservatism. I don't think anybody should enter a marriage they later regret. And I never have.

On Living Alone

IT'S SUNDAY morning, and I'm walking up Columbus Avenue. Couples are coming at me on all sides. They
fill the street from building line to pavement edge. Some
are clasped together looking raptly into each other's
faces; some are holding hands, their eyes restless,
window-shopping; some walk side by side, stony faced,
carefully not touching. I have the sudden conviction
that half these people will, in a few months, be walking
with someone else now walking on the avenue as one
half of another couple. Eventually that arrangement
will terminate as well, and each man and each woman
will once again be staring out the window of a room
empty of companionship. This is a population in a per-
manent state of intermittent attachment. Inevitably, the
silent apartment lies in wait.

Who could ever have dreamed there would be so

many of us floating around, those of us between thirty-five and fifty-five who live alone. Thirty years of politics in the street opened a door that became a floodgate, and we have poured through in our monumental numbers, in possession of the most educated discontent in history. Yet, we seem puzzled, most of us, about how we got here, confused and wanting relief from the condition. We roam the crowded streets, in naked expectation of the last-minute reprieve. For us, human density is a requirement. Density alone provides material for the perpetual regrouping that is our necessity.

THE WAY I SEE IT, I said yes to this and no to that, and found myself living alone. I never *did* understand that response itself is choice. For years, mine were strongly influenced only by what I took to be a grand concern: I was on my guard against the fear of loneliness. It seemed important to me that I sort out the issues of life—work and love—without securing against the terrors of a solitary old age. Fear of loneliness, I maintained, had been responsible for so many unholy bargains made by so many women that fighting the anxiety became something of a piece of politics for me. A position I took with ease, as my understanding of the matter was primitive.

I married in my mid-twenties. My husband and I had been friends, but once married we became rapidly locked into other people's ideas of a husband and a wife. One day we were a pair of serious-minded students putting our small meals on the table together, taking turns washing up, doing the laundry. The next day I was alone in the kitchen with a cookbook while he read the paper in the living room; when he looked up it was to speculate aloud, in the direction of the kitchen, about his work, our future. I grew alarmed, and so did he. Our alarm filled the apartment and became a bane of existence. This bane held our attention to a morbid degree. We seemed continuously to be brooding on why we were not happy.

We thought of ourselves as enlightened people. The idea had been to go forward into life side by side, facing outward, at the world, but now we found that we faced only inward, each toward the ignorant other. Slowly, the relationship that was meant to serve our lives became our life. The more uncertain we grew the more we protested that love was everything. Nothing, we said, was to come between us and our love. We two would be as one. That was the norm. Deviation from the norm could only unnerve and unsettle.

This policy did not take us to the promised land, it led us further out into the desert. Neither of us, it seemed, was to be allowed an independent impulse. It became habitual for one or the other to complain regularly, "How can you say you love me and want to do *that*?" Inevitably, what either he or I had wanted to do that so outraged the other was gratify an interest that served only our own separate selves, a desire the other experienced as excluding and therefore disloyal. But the restriction went against nature: The impulse kept surfacing, like a weed pushing up through concrete.

Grieving over failed intimacy (the shock and the abnormality of it), our unhappiness seemed shameful (here we were, married and more alone than when alone). Shame isolates. The isolation was humiliating. Humiliation does not bear thinking about. We began to concentrate on not thinking.

The more troubled our attachment became the more time we spent in each other's company. We were always together. It wasn't that we enjoyed being together, not at all, it was simply that we could not bear to be apart. Together, we generated tension, but alone we each fell into an intense loneliness. The loneliness was more painful than the tension, to be avoided at any cost. Eventually, if I said I was going to the store for a container of milk my husband said he'd walk along with me. The people we knew—they were all as young as we—said, Look how devoted they are. It was marriage that taught me anxiety looks like devotion, and loneliness is the human condition most rejecting of easy analysis.

The obsession with avoiding ourselves became degrading. Our own emotions were now the enemy. A protective shell grew up around all feeling. When this shell thickened the flesh at the center shriveled. Young and healthy, I felt buried alive.

At last we parted.

I REMEMBER lying in bed that first morning staring up at the small square of bedroom ceiling. I remember the sunny silence and the bliss I felt at not having to respond to: anyone. Peace, utter peace: the shadows gone, the anxiety cleared out. What remained was open space. My presence filled the tiny apartment. I stood naked in the middle of the room. I yawned and I stretched. The *idea* of love seemed an invasion. I had thoughts to think, a craft to learn, a self to discover. Solitude was a gift. A world was waiting to welcome me if I was willing to enter it alone. I put on my clothes and walked through the door.

It was the early seventies, an exciting time, and a great many women shared the excitement. We had become converts to the woman's movement. When we met, all of us, in public places, coming together again and again for the pleasure of elaborating the insight and repeating the analysis, the world expanded into an extended companionateness of extraordinary dimension. This companionateness exhilarated and sustained. Coming home from a meeting I experienced my rooms as warm and welcoming, the orderliness and the quiet a pleasure and a relief, the conversation still buzzing in my head. There was no one in the room but me, and I was far from alone. I had brought home company, wonderful company, company that gave me back myself.

But the closeness was a function of the moment— that moment when feminism had felt revolutionary— and when the moment passed, the comradeliness passed with it. Then it was as though I knew a great many people, but none of them knew each other. The illusion of an integrated life evaporated. It was back to urban social life as I had known it before my marriage: fragmented and highly strung, marked by the tensions and withdrawals of exacerbated lives and personalities, friendships that were always in and out of phase. Without domestic companionship, it startled me to see, daily connection was by no means a given.

One day I realized I was alone, not only in the apartment but in the world. If I didn't pick up that phone and make at least one call. . . . And even when I did pick up the phone, the times without number when, no matter how many calls I made, everyone was occupied, no one was available. . . . The quiet pressed in on me. The apartment resonated with its own silence. The silence deepened. Solitude was now problematic.

Loneliness, when it came, came—then as now—like a surge of physical illness. It began with a pressure behind the eyes that forced a frown onto my face. In a matter of minutes I'd be struck down, sick and sweating, misery washing through my chest, fear radiating out in waves from the pit of my stomach. I'd lie down on the couch with an open book in my hands and wait for the seizure to pass. Sometimes, though, it would go on for days, especially in the warm and dreamy seasons of the year. I can recall a thousand mornings when I've awakened into the piercing sweetness of a summer day feeling as though my bed was anchored to a gray, unpeopled landscape, while just outside the window the world is bathed in a fluid element and all the people in it are splashing about, brilliant with color, in pairs and in groups.

So here I was, no longer alone and pleased to be alone, now alone and in pain. I did the obvious then: made

those phone calls, went wherever I was invited, cultivated acquaintanceships indiscriminately; and shortly,
if I wished, I could be out every night of the week.
When mere sociability became intolerable, I'd give myself a little lecture on the former joys of solitude, urging
myself to spend the evening reading as I had done so frequently throughout the years of my life. Then I'd lie
down on the couch, barely getting through fifty pages in
three hours, reading the same sentence three times before its content was absorbed, but on the couch all the
same, toughing it out.

Pain produced insight and energy but not balance or
detachment. Getting through a lonely evening like a patient surmounting a fever, and praising myself for not
succumbing to the worst excesses of self-pity, was surely
not a sign of indomitable spirit. If that was the best I
could do, I might as well get married! At those words my
back stiffened. I'd be damned and gone to hell first. I saw
that more was involved here than a simple matter of
pleasure or pain. I had begun to have a stake in living
alone.

I wrote a polemic called "Against Marriage." In this
piece I argued that we marry not for the adventure of
self-discovery or a shared inner life, but for emotional
solace of a primitive sort. What comes with the solace
is insularity, an amateurish relation to solitude, and hard
questions about the inner self that go unasked for years
at a time. Fear of loneliness, I said, is at the heart of the
matter. To secure against a fear one must move into it,
live with it, face it down. To live without love or domes-

tic intimacy, I generously allowed, was indeed to be
half-alive but, I concluded, what we want now is to be
real to ourselves. The myth of two-shall-become-as-
one is no longer useful. Living consciously is the business of our lives. If one cannot win over loneliness, at
least one can learn that it's not fatal. Such knowledge becomes a strength, an ally, a weapon.

Writing these thoughts into articles and essays became my comfort and my necessity. To write clearly on
the subject, I felt, was to be renewed if not redeemed. I
did not notice the rhetoric riding these pages, swelling
their sentences, confining thought. I had persuaded myself that to write the problem out was to put it behind
me . . . and not only me. The piece produced an uproar.
I was challenged on a dozen scores, and I replied on all
of them. In my own ears the replies were reasonable, but
the more I explained the more entrenched I became.
Before I knew it, an insight had become a theory, a theory a position, a position a dogma.

I was a born ideologue: I thrived on having a position.
Now I had one: To live alone is to face down loneliness.
It became a litany that in the bad times strengthened me,
gave me stamina and self-control. No need to review its
contents. All I had to do was keep repeating the mantra.

Years passed (that's what they did: they passed).
Things remained in place. Then suddenly, without
warning or consent, I was thrown back on my own
dogma, and after that nothing was in place. Teaching in
a southern university town, I met a woman my own age,
divorced with grown children away at school. She sug-

gested I share a house with her. I thought her a sympathetic soul and decided, after years of living alone, to
chance it.

I had stumbled into a remarkably compatible arrangement. Between me and this woman there were
no moods, tensions, depressions, or withdrawals. We
seemed never to bore, irritate, or intrude on each other.
We conducted our daily lives independently, yet were
always delighted to spend an evening at home together.
Conversation was an ever deepening pleasure between
us, but neither of us ever made the other feel guilty for
wanting to be alone. In short, the relationship was sim-
plicity itself, and it provided us both with the joys of civ-
ilized friendship and domestic tranquillity, a condition
of life I had never known.

What took me by surprise was the relief I felt at not
living alone. The relief and the gratitude. After all, what
was happening here? I wasn't with a lover or even with
an intimate friend. I was simply sharing a house with a
compatible person. I had the pleasure of coffee in the
morning and a chat in the evening with a woman I enjoyed talking with and the comfort of knowing we
spent the night under the same roof. It was an absence of
gross loneliness that was having an extraordinary effect
on me.

And it *was* extraordinary. To begin with, I felt calm
every day and all through the day—deeply calm. I realized from this calm that ordinarily I sustain, and probably have for years, a kind of low-grade anxiety that seeps
daily into the nervous system. Nothing to get excited

about, certainly nothing I can't handle, but it's a *feeling* I have, one I had stopped registering and would not again have been aware of if it weren't for this superb calm that now came bubbling up in me a couple of times a day.

Along with the calm, I felt smoothed out inside, as though some great blue-and-white wave had cleaned me down, washing away the grit. It was then I realized I feel gritty inside, all the time. Again, nothing to get excited about, nothing that can't be handled. Just there it was. Loneliness feels gritty.

Then the fog in my head—always a shred of it floating here or there—seemed to clear out. I found myself concentrating for hours, instead of minutes, at a time. I hadn't realized until that moment how continually my attention is being shredded, the worried granulation of inner clarity that is my constant companion.

I looked around then, at my life, and I saw that I had not learned to live alone at all. What I had learned to do was strategize; lie down until the pain passed; evade; get by. I wasn't drowning, but I wasn't swimming either. I was floating on my back, far from shore, waiting to be saved.

Looking closely at a condition that hadn't been reviewed in years, I saw that once again the thing was being named; the thing I knew and had forgotten times without number; the thing that each time I name I make more my own but each time I forget makes me lose ground. I found myself remembering the time long ago when I had first understood the thing I would always forget. It was also the day I understood why I walk, why

I am a walker in the city. The memory materialized so powerfully that suddenly the day was standing before me:

I had been wandering around the apartment for hours, avoiding the desk. Couldn't think, couldn't write. My head filling up with fog, mist, cotton wool, dry ice; the fog rolling in through the window tops. The usual. The daily experience. The condition I struggle with from nine in the morning on, fighting to occupy a small clear space in my head until two or three in the afternoon when I desert the effort, feeling empty and defeated and as if I haven't heard the sound of a human voice in a thousand years.

That afternoon I had an appointment uptown, at an address three miles from my house, and on impulse I decided to walk. When I hit the street it was as though I'd emerged from a cave into the light. Everything I saw—shops, lights, cars, people—looked interesting to me. I took a deep breath and felt my lungs swell. Then I ran into someone I hadn't seen in years. The exhilaration of the unexpected encounter! My stride lengthened. I got where I was going, did what I'd gone to do, and decided to walk back. When I got home I saw that the bad feeling had washed out of me. I was purged. The walk had purged me.

I realized then how ordinary my depression was. Ordinary and predictable, ordinary and daily. Daily depression, that's all it was. I saw, as though for the first time, that daily depression eats energy. Without energy inner life evaporates; without inner life there is no animation; without animation there is no work. A life in thrall to daily depression is doomed to mediocrity.

In the same moment I saw that *this* was loneliness, the thing itself. Loneliness was the evaporation of inner life. Loneliness was me cut off from myself. Loneliness was the thing nothing out there could cure.

The depression was, I knew, rooted in a grievance that was old, older than love, older than marriage, older than friendship or politics. The grievance was my dear friend, my close friend. I had given up many others over the years, but not this one, never this one. This one, I saw, had been given the run of the house.

I knew enough to know that I would not hold on to what I was now seeing: that something in me would refuse to absorb the information. I would forget. I would not take it in. I would be overwhelmed again. Insight alone could not save me. I'd have to clear out each day anew. Walking had purged me, washed me clean, but only for that day. I understood the dailiness of the task. I was condemned to walk.

More important, I was condemned to live with what I could not take in.

We all were. Those of us who live alone, treading water, waiting for a pardon, clinging to the most educated discontent in history.

I WALK UP Columbus Avenue with new respect for life in a solitary state. I look into the avid, searching faces and I think, How well we are doing here in the brutal filthy city, those of us who stare out the window of a room empty of companionship, with the taste of grit in the morning coffee, low-grade anxiety in the evening drink. Out there, in America, our faces are withdrawn and remote, made eccentric by isolation. On Columbus Avenue collective loneliness is a stable element. It has culture-making properties.

Here: Grace

Y O U W I L L love me?" my husband asks, and at something in his tone my consciousness rouses like a startled cat, ears pricked, pupils round and onyx-black.

Never voluble, he has been unusually subdued this evening. Thinking him depressed about the mysterious symptoms that have plagued him for months and that we know in our heart of hearts signal a recurrence of cancer, although the tests won't confirm it for several more days, I pressed up against him on the couch and whispered against his neck, "This may be the most troublesome time of our lives, but I'm so happy." This awareness of joy, though it's been growing for several years now, has recently expanded in response to my own failing health. A few weeks ago, pondering the possibility that I might die at any time, I posed myself a new question: *If I died at this very moment, would I die happy?* And the answer burst out without hesitation: *Yes!* Since then, in spite of my fears, I've felt a new contentment. What more could I ever ask than to give an unequivocal response to such a question?

His silence persisted. "Scared?" I asked him after a few moments, thinking of the doctor's appointment that morning, the CAT scan scheduled for later in the week. Head resting on the back of the couch, eyes closed, he nodded. More silence. Finally I said, "George, you know how I love words. I need words!"

And now, words: "You will love me?" Behind his glasses, his eyes have the startled look I associate, incongruously, with the moment of orgasm.

"Yes," I tell him, alert, icy all over. "I can safely promise you that. I will always love you."

"You asked the other day whether my illness could be AIDS," he says unevenly. "I'm pretty sure it isn't, because I had the test for HIV some time ago, after I had an affair for a couple of years with another woman."

The sensation is absolutely nonverbal, but everybody knows it even without words: the stunned breathlessness that follows a jab to the solar plexus. What will astonish me in the days to come is that this sensation can sustain itself long after one would expect to be dead of asphyxiation. I have often wished myself dead. If it were possible to die of grief, I would die at this moment. But it's not, and I don't.

A couple of years. *A couple of years.* This was no fit of passion, no passing fancy, but a sustained commitment. He loved her, loves her still: Their relationship, until he

broke it off—for reasons having little to do with me—
was a kind of marriage, he says. Time after time after
time he went to her, deliberately, telling whatever lies
he needed to free himself from me and the children, and
later from his mother when she came for a protracted
visit after his father's death, throughout at least a couple
of years.

More. He'd fallen in love with her six years earlier, I
could sense at that time, and they'd had a prolonged flir-
tation. She was a bitter, brittle woman, and something
about her rage inflamed him. Their paths had parted,
however, and I had no way of knowing of their later
chance encounter, courtship, years-long "marriage."
And after that ended—here, in this room, which will
ever hereafter be haunted by her tears—four years of silence: too late to tell me, he says, and then too later, and
then too later still. Twelve of our twenty-seven years of
marriage suddenly called, one way or another, into
question. I recall my brother's description of his framing
shop after the San Francisco earthquake, how miracu-
lously nothing in it was broken, not even the sheets of
glass for covering pictures, but it looked as though some
giant gremlin had come in and slid everything a few feet
to one side. My past feels similarly shoved out of whack,
not shattered but strangely reconfigured, and out of its
shadows steps a man I have never seen before: Sandra's
lover.

IF I WERE that proverbial virtuous woman, the one
whose price is far above rubies, perhaps I would have the

right to order George out of my sight, out of my house, out of my life. But I'm not that woman. I'm the other one, the one whose accusers dropped their stones and skulked away. I've desired other men, slept with them, even loved them, although I've never felt married to one. I guess I took my girlhood vow literally: I have always thought of marriage as something one did once and forever. All the same, in brief passionate bursts I've transgressed the sexual taboos that give definition to Christian marriage.

I'm not a virtuous woman, but I am a candid one. Many years ago, George and I pledged that we would not again lie to anyone about anything. I haven't been strictly faithful to the spirit of this promise, either, because I've deliberately withheld information on occasion (although not, according to my mother, often enough, having an unfortunate propensity for spilling the family beans in print); but I have not, when directly challenged, lied. This commitment can have maddening consequences: One night I listened for half an hour or longer to the outpourings of a total stranger in response to an essay in one of my books because I couldn't tell her that I had a pot on the stove about to boil over when I actually didn't. Had Daddy and I meant that vow for *everybody,* my daughter asked after I hung up the telephone, not just for each other? Not even, I can see now, for each other: especially not for each other.

"How can you ever believe me again after this?" George asks, and I shrug: "I've believed you all this time. I'm in the habit of it. Why should I stop now?" And so I go on believing him, but a subtle difference will emerge over time: belief becomes a matter of faith, no longer logically connected to the "truth" of its object, which remains unknowable except insofar as it chooses to reveal itself. I suppose I could hire a private detective to corroborate George's tales, but I'm not going to because George's whereabouts are no less his own business now than they ever were. I can envision some practical difficulties in my being unable to locate him at any given time, but no moral ones, whereas I perceive a serious problem in seeking information that would curb his freedom to lie, a freedom without which he can't freely tell me the truth. I don't want to come by my belief through extortion. Once, I believed George because it never occurred to me not to believe him; now I believe him because I prefer belief, which affirms his goodness, to doubt, which sneers and sniggers at it. No longer an habitual response, belief becomes an act of love.

It does not thereby absolve George of responsibility for the choices he has freely made, however. The years while he was slipping away to sleep with Sandra were among the most wretched of my not conspicuously cheerful life; and by lying to me, he permitted—no, really encouraged—me to believe that my unhappiness was, as always, my own fault, even though, thanks to the wonders of psychopharmacology, I was at last no longer clinically depressed. I remember lying awake, night after night, while he stayed up late grading papers and then dropped into bed, and instantly into sleep, without a word or a touch; as he twitched and snored, I'd prowl

through the dark house, sip milk or wine, smoke cigarettes, write in my journal until, shuddering with cold
and loneliness, I'd be forced to creep back into bed. Past
forty, he must have been conserving his sexual energies,
I realize now, but when I expressed concern and sadness,
he blamed our chilling relationship on me: I was dis-
tracted, too bitchy, not affectionate enough. . . . Ah, he
knew my self-doubts thoroughly.

Breakdowns in our relationship, especially sexual
ones, had habitually been ascribed to me. "I'm very
tired," I wrote in my journal early in this period of misery, twenty years into our marriage, "of his putting me
down all the time—telling me that I'm too involved
with Anne, that I don't handle Matthew well, that I'm
not affectionate (the only signs of affection he recog-
nizes are physical, which I suppose makes sense, since he
doesn't communicate verbally). In short, that I'm a bad
mother and wife. I just don't know how to feel much
affection for someone I feel sorry for, for being married
to me." Tired of disparagement I may already have been,
but I took over two years more to recognize myself as a
collaborator in it: "He survives—thrives—on my cul-
pability. Without it, where would he be today? We've
both built our lives on it, and if I remove it, our relationship will no longer have any foundation."

This awareness of complicity precipitated out of a
homely crisis (the form of most of my crises), in the
winter of 1985, involving the proper setting of the thermostat, which George persistently left at sixty degrees
even though I couldn't bear the temperature below

sixty-five (and, as came out in the course of the dispute, neither could he). When I told him that the coldness of the house represented my growing feelings of neglect and abandonment, he countered that he had to go elsewhere (leaving the thermostat set at sixty) in order to get the touching and affection he needed. It was, I noted, "the same old ploy, trying to trigger my guilt for not being a physically affectionate wife. Only this time I could feel myself not quite biting. Because he wants the physical part to continue regardless of the pain I'm in, even if he causes the pain, and he blames me if I won't put out, come across, what have you. And I'm sick unto death of bearing the blame." He could, I suddenly understood, turn up the heat himself. He chose not to.

Or rather, he chose to turn it up in some other woman's house. In spite of the sexual stresses underlying this controversy, he gave no hint that his longing for "warmth and light" was taking him from the crumbling converted Chinese grocery where the children and I lived to a spacious, immaculate, perfectly appointed home in a tranquil neighborhood miles away; and I didn't guess. Just as he knew how to exploit my self-doubts, he knew how to escape me. Teaching in two programs, he was out of the house from at least eight-thirty in the morning until eight-thirty at night; he devoted his spare time to good works like cooking at Casa María soup kitchen, observing the federal trial of the people who had arranged sanctuary for refugees from El Salvador, and editing *¡Presente!,* the local Catholics for

Peace and Justice newsletter. With such a schedule, of course he'd have little enough energy left for sex, or even a leisurely family dinner. Another woman (his lover, for instance) might have judged his devotion to illiterate, poor, and oppressed people sanctimonious, even morbid, but I found it natural and necessary.

As a result, he put me in a conscientious bind: I felt abandoned, and I believed that George was neglecting our troubled teenaged son dangerously, but I couldn't make our needs weigh heavily enough against those of five hundred empty bellies at the kitchen door or a Salvadoran woman who'd fled her village in terror when the last of her sons disappeared. Still, I wondered uneasily why the spiritual growth he said he was seeking necessitated his setting out on what appeared to be "a quest—Galahad and the Holy Grail—noble and high-minded and above all out there, beyond the muck and mire of daily living in a decaying house with a crippled wife and a rebellious adolescent son." Forced to let him go, I did so with a bitter blessing: "Feed the poor, my dear. Shelter the refugees. Forget the impoverishment you leave in your wake. It's only Nancy and Matthew and Anne, after all—nothing spiritual there, nothing uplifting, no real needs, just niggling demands that drag at you, cling to you, slow your lofty ascent into the light and life of Christ."

Our approaches to ministry were hopelessly at odds: "I think that the life of Christ is only this life, which one must enter further and further. And I hate the entering.

I'd give anything to escape. . . . There's no glamor here, no glory. Only the endless grading of papers. The being present for two difficult children. The making of another meal. The dragging around of an increasingly crippled body, forcing it to one end of the house and back again, out the door, into the classroom, home again, up from the bed, up from the toilet, up from the couch. The extent of my lofty ascent. I want only to do what I must with as much grace as I can." That George, finding these conditions squalid and limiting, sought to minister elsewhere embittered but hardly surprised me. And so, whenever he wanted Sandra, he had only to murmur "Soup. Sanctuary. *¡Presente!*" in order to be as free of them as he liked.

I have been, it appears, a bit of a fool. "Where did I think you'd gone?" I ask George. "What lies did I believe?" He claims not to remember. He will always claim not to remember such details, which is his prerogative, but the writer in me obsessively scribbles in all the blanks he leaves. I imagine the two of them sitting half-naked beside her pool, sipping cold Coronas and laughing at my naïveté, and then I have to laugh myself: I would have been the last thing on their minds. This sense of my own extinction will prove the most tenacious and terrifying of my responses, the one that keeps me flat on my back in the night, staring into the dark, gasping for breath, as though I've been buried alive. For almost thirty years, except during a couple of severe disintegrative episodes, my presence to George has kept me present to myself. Now, at just the moment when cancer threatens to remove that reassurance of my own reality from my future, it's yanked from my past as well. Throughout his sweet stolen hours with Sandra, George lived where I was not.

"Aʀᴇ ʏᴏᴜ all right?" my daughter asks on the day following George's revelation when she stumbles upon me huddled in my studio, rocking and shivering. I shake my head. "Shall I cut class and stay here with you?"

"No, go to class," I say. "Then come back. We'll talk."

"You're not going to do anything rash while I'm gone?" It's the question of a child seasoned in suicide, and I wish she didn't have to ask it.

"I promise. Scoot."

I hadn't planned to tell Anne, at least not yet; but George is getting sicker by the day, his mother is about to arrive for several weeks, Christmas is coming, and I don't think I can deal with this new complication alone. I have George's permission to tell whomever I wish. "I want you to write about this," he says. "I want you to write about us." For himself, he has never revealed it to anyone except once, early on, the psychotherapist with whom we've worked, together and apart, over the years. But he believes in the value of what I try to do in my work: in reclaiming human experience, insofar as I can find it embodied in my own experience, from the morass of secrecy and shame into which Christian and pre-Christian social taboos have plunged it, to rescue and restore God's good creation. (And if at times the work proves as smelly as pumping a septic tank, well, shit is God's creation, too.) George supports it, but the work itself is mine. If any bad tidings are to be borne, I am the one to bear them.

"But Mom," Anne says when I've finished my tale of woe, "men *do* these things." Transcribed, these words might look like a twenty-five-year-old's cynicism, but in fact her tone rings purely, and characteristically, pragmatic. It's just the tone I need to jerk my attention back from private misery to the human condition. She's right, of course. In the Judaic roots of our culture, as Uta Ranke-Heinemann points out in *Eunuchs for the Kingdom of Heaven*, "a man could never violate his own marriage. The wife belonged to her husband, but the husband did not belong to his wife," and a couple of thousand years of Church teaching on the subject of marital fidelity—not all of it a model of clarity and consistency—has never entirely balanced the expectations placed on the two partners. *People* do these things, Anne means (I know: I have done them myself); but ordinary men, men possessed of healthy sexual appetites, have been tacitly *entitled* to do them. They're just *like* that.

Except for my man. One reviewer of my first book of essays, *Plaintext*, wrote: "The reader will also wish to see more closely some of the people who simply drift through these essays, especially Mairs' husband, who comes across as a saint, staying through extreme mood swings, suicide attempts, severe illness, and a number of love affairs." That's *my* man: a saint. Through my essays I've publicly canonized him. Any man who could stay

with a crazy, crippled, unfaithful bitch like me had to
be more than humanly patient and loving and long-
suffering and self-abnegating and . . . oh, just more
than human. ,

Admittedly, I had help in forming this view, especially from other women; a man whose bearing is as
gentle and courtly as George's can seem a true miracle,
one my inconstancy plainly didn't merit. "But hasn't
he ever slept with another woman?" more than one person has asked, and I've said proudly, gratefully, "No. I've
asked him, and he tells me he never has." I often told myself that he "ought to go, get out now, while he's still
fairly young, find a healthy woman free from black
spells, have some fun. No one could blame him." And
occasionally, trying to account for his physical and emotional unavailability, I'd conjecture: "Perhaps another
woman—he's so attractive and romantic that that
thought always crosses my mind." My guess was dead
on, it turns out, formed at the height of his affair with
just the sort of healthy woman I'd had in mind, but I
took him at his word and felt humbled—humiliated—
that he had responded to my infidelities with such
steadfastness.

A saint's wife readily falls prey to self-loathing, I discovered, since comparisons are both common and invidious, and recuperation, if it occurs at all, is a protracted and lonely process. One evening a couple of
years ago, when I'd been invited to discuss *Plaintext* with
a local women's reading group and the conversation
turned, as such conversations always seem to, to my in-

fidelity and George's forbearance, I blurted: "Wait a minute! Did it ever occur to you that there might be some advantage to being married to the woman who wrote *Plaintext*?" At last I'd reached the point where I could ask that question. But as I sipped coffee and nibbled a chocolate cookie in the company of these polite and pleasant but plainly distressed strangers, my chances of getting an affirmative answer seemed as remote as ever. In this tale, I was decidedly not the Princess but the Dragon.

George has conspired in his own sanctification. Why wouldn't he? The veneration of others must be seductive. And if, in order to perpetuate it, he had to affirm—to me, and through me to others familiar with my writings—his faithfulness even as he shuttled between Sandra and me, well, what harm was he doing? For her own reasons, Sandra was just as eager as he to keep the affair clandestine. They seldom went out and never got together with friends; he never even encountered her child, who was always, magically, "not there"; she'd even meet him in a parking lot and drive him to her house so that the neighbors wouldn't see his car. He could maintain this oddly hermetic relationship without risk to the sympathy and admiration of friends, family, and book reviewers alike. No one need ever know.

Until, ultimately, me. That is, I don't need to know, not at all, I've done very well indeed without knowing, but he has come to need to tell me. At first, he thought merely breaking with Sandra would calm the dread his father's death and the discovery of melanoma in a lymph

node stirred in him, but now he needs a stronger remedy. "I feel this awful blackness inside. I just want to die,"
he says after confessing, and I shudder, because an awful blackness is precisely what he has inside—a six-
centimeter melanoma attached to his small bowel—and
I don't want him to die, he can tell me anything, I'll accept whatever he confesses, any number of awful black-
nesses, if only please he won't die. He hasn't any control
over that, alas, but at least now he has cleared his conscience thoroughly. I think he's after another clarity as
well, one that involves putting off sainthood and standing naked—bones jutting under wasted flesh, scars
puckering arm and belly, penis too limp now for love—
as a man. He wants to be loved as he is, not as we—his
mother, my mother, my sisters, our daughter, his students, our friends, maybe even Sandra herself—have
dreamed him. I most of all. I look anew at the reviewer's
words: "The reader will wish to *see more closely* some of
the people who *simply drift* through these essays. . . . "

George is accustomed to holding himself slightly
aloof. The only child of adoring parents, he grew up believing himself entitled to act on his own desires without regard for the needs of others: There weren't any
others. If he wanted the last cookie, it was his. (In fact,
even if he didn't want it, his mother probably made him
take it.) No noisy wrangles, no division of the coveted
cookie followed by wails that "he got the bigger half,"
no snitching a bite while the other's head was turned or
spitting on the other's half to spoil it for both, just com-
placent munching down to the last sweet crumb. But,

by the same token, no whispers and giggles under the covers after Mother has put out the light *for absolutely the last time.* No shared cookies. No shared secrets, either. No entanglements, true. But no intimacy.

Having grown up in an extensive family linked by complicated affections, with a slightly younger sister who still sometimes seems hooked into my flesh, I don't think I ever quite comprehended George's implacable self-sufficiency. Maybe for that reason I allowed, even encouraged, his remoteness. And I did. The reviewer is talking, after all, not about George's nature but about my essays. If the reader wants to "see" George "more closely," then I have not seen him closely enough. George "drifts" through my essays because I permitted him to drift through my life. "I couldn't imagine," he tells me now, "that what I was doing, as long as I kept it in a separate little box, had any effect on the rest of you." Like his indulgent mother, I let him persist in such manly detachment. I'd have served him better as a scrappy sister.

What I might have thought of, in good aging-hippy fashion, as "giving him space," letting him "do his own thing," strikes me now as a failure of love. Respecting another's freedom does not require cutting him loose and letting him drift; the lines of love connecting us one to another are stays, not shackles. I do not want to fail again. After the children and I have each spoken with him separately about the affair, I say to him: "You may have hoped, in confessing to us, that we'd punish you by sending you away, but now you see that we won't do that. If you want to leave, you'll have to go on your own initiative. As far as we're concerned, you're not an only child, you're one of us. We love you. We intend, if you will let us, to keep you."

You will love me?" George asked at the beginning of this terrible test, and I find, to my relief, that I can keep my promise. "But can you forgive him?" asks our friend Father Ricardo when we seek his counsel, and I reply, without hesitation, "I already have."

I *have*? How can this be? I have never felt more hurt than I do now. I am angry. I am bitter. I try to weep but my eyes feel blasted, although occasionally I shudder and gasp in some stone's version of crying its heart out. I dread going out into the city for fear I'll encounter Sandra. I torment myself with images of George pressing his lips to hers, stroking her hair, slowly unbuttoning her blouse, calling her "sweetheart," too. *She got the sex*, I reflect sardonically as I keep my vigil through surgery and its horrific aftermath, then through chemotherapy, *and I get the death*. I despise her for her willingness to risk my marriage without a thought; and yet in a queer way I pity her because, as it has turned out, she has to live without George and, for the moment, I do not.

Worst of all, ghastly congratulatory cheers ring in my head: *Good-o, George! You've finally given the bitch her comeuppance: tit for tat, an eye for an eye, and not a whit more than she deserves.* "What do you care what people think?" he shrugs when I tell him of this fantastic taunting, but the truth is that, with new comprehension of the suffering my adultery must have caused him, I'm

tempted to join the chorus. Still, although our affairs
may be connected chronologically (mine all took place
before his) and causally (bitterness about mine offered
him permission for his), morally they stand separate. I
don't merit the pain I'm now in, any more than George
ever deserved to be hurt, but we have unquestionably
wounded each other horribly and we each bear full
moral responsibility for the other's pain. George is right
to dismiss my demonic chorus: What matters is not
mockery and blame, whether our own or others', but
mutual contrition. Over and over when he clings to me
and weeps as I cannot and says, "I'm sorry, I'm sorry," I
hold him, stroking his back and murmuring reassur-
ances: that I love him, that I'll be all right, that he hasn't
"spoiled" us, that through this pain we can grow. Forgiveness is not even in question. It is simply, mysteri-
ously, already accomplished.

Week after week he has stood beside me telling me
what I have not wanted to know: *I confess to Almighty
God, and to you, my brothers and sisters, that I have sinned,
through my own fault, in my thoughts and in my words, in
what I have done and in what I have failed to do.* Now that
he's divulged the specific contents of his conscience to
me, I'm curious what this little ritual of general confession meant during the time he so plainly wasn't sorry for
what he was doing. "Did you ever think about Sandra as
you said those words?" I ask. "Did you think what you
were doing might be wrong?"

"Well, yes, I knew it was. But I also knew I didn't intend to stop. So I just had to hope that God had a sense of

humor." Fortunately for George, God has a much better sense of humor than I do. But I've been working on it. Meanwhile, week after week his voice has spoken aloud at my side: *And I ask Blessed Mary ever virgin, all the angels and saints, and you, my brothers and sisters, to pray for me to the Lord our God.* As bidden, I have prayed for him, as for myself and for all the disembodied voices floating up behind me, that God might have mercy on us, forgive us our sins, and lead each one of us to everlasting life. Believing myself forgiven by God, I must believe George equally forgiven. And if forgiven by God, surely no less by me.

One of the elements that drew me into the Catholic Church was the concept of grace, although I've never been able to make more than clumsy sense of it. I am moved by the idea that God always already loves us first, before we love God, wholly and without condition, that God forgives us even before we have done anything to require forgiveness, as we will inevitably do, and that this outpouring of love and forgiveness fortifies us for repentance and reform. I am moved—but not persuaded. I am simply incapable of grasping an abstraction unless I can root it experientially, and nothing in my experience has revealed quite how grace works. Until now. The uncontingent love and forgiveness I feel for George, themselves a gift of grace, unwilled and irresistible, intimate that grace whose nature has eluded me.

For the most theologically unsophisticated of reasons, involving a dead father who went, I was told, to heaven up in the sky, together with continual reiterations, from about the same age on, of "Our Father, who art in heaven . . . ," I always expect spiritual insights to shower like coins of light from on high. When instead they bubble up from the mire like will-o'-the-wisps, I am invariably startled. Grace *here*, among these lies and shattered vows, sleepless nights, remorse, recriminations? Yes, precisely, here: Grace.

But forgiveness does not, whatever the aphorism says, entail forgetfulness. Never mind the sheer impossibility of forgetting that your husband has just told you he's had an affair, a strenuous version of that childhood game in which you try, on a dare, *not* to think about a three-legged green cat licking persimmon marmalade from the tip of its tail. Never mind memory's malarial tenacity, the way that, weeks and months and even years after you think the shock has worn off, as you recall a trip you made to Washington to receive a writing award, it occurs to you that in your absence they may have made love for the first time and all your words, the ones you'd written before and the ones you've written since, shrivel and scatter like ashes. Never mind.

Mind what matters: his presence here, for now. Love is not love, forgiveness is not forgiveness, that effaces the beloved's lineaments by letting him drift, indistinct, through the lives of those who claim him. That way lies lethargy, which is the death of love. I am not married to Saint George, after all. I am married to a man who is, among many other things neither more nor less remarkable, an adulterer. I must remember him: whole.

An Exile's Psalm

THE SOUTH FLORIDA night is glossy, dark, and fragrant; it smells of roots and leaves, salt and the swamp, a not unpleasant whiff of septic tank. Over Highway One is a startlingly brilliant swath of stars. We recognize, out over the dark expanse of water, Orion and the Big Dipper high up in the space defined by the windshield of our rental car. It's early January and Paul and I have been traveling nearly all day; we've flown into Miami and rented this little metallic-blue Escort a few shades darker than the sea. We're on the way to a writers' conference in Key West, where I'm teaching first thing in the morning, so even though it's after midnight we keep driving, following the unlikely curve of the causeway as it flings itself from island to narrow island. One of the bridges claims to be seven miles long. I know we're missing out on the famous blue-green water (the sort of color Elizabeth Bishop described as "pistachio green and Mermaid Milk"), but I'm glad it's dark so I'm less aware of driving on an unspooling ribbon of concrete a dozen yards above the ocean.

We're as exhilarated as we are tired, and we stop often to take in where we are, or as much of where we are as we can apprehend in the dark. One of our greatest pleasures is traveling together, and it's especially welcome to find ourselves someplace warm and moist, geographically and spiritually far from the snowy winter we've been trundling through. We pull off along the shoulder of the road and look at the lights of boats candling in the distance, the only evidence of just how far to either side the sea goes on. We wander through a deserted late-night grocery on Key Largo which offers, among the plantains and globes of grapefruit in the produce section, the stuffed heads of alligators, mounted on wooden plaques, their glass eyes managing to look both desperate and indifferent at once.

Then, on Big Pine Key, a marvel. Along the road, signs announce a thirty-five-mile-per-hour night speed limit because the area is a protected habitat for an endangered species, the tiny key deer. Paul says in all the time he's spent in Florida he's never seen them, so I assume we'll just drive slowly past dark groves of shrubbery in which the exotic creatures must be hiding. But right by the side of the road, a herd of small dun-colored shapes materialize in our headlights; we stop the car as we realize what we're seeing. A buck's poised right beside us, his marvelous little cluster of antlers—an upside-down chandelier—bunched close together. He seems to be standing sentinel for the does, who graze just down the grassy slope (a grim notion, to think the road provides a lure for them). Because we're sitting in a low-slung vehicle, we're at eye-level with the buck, who's all of three feet tall and blinking at us with a kind of calm which it's hard not to read as benevolent and self-assured. He's entirely unperturbed.

This is the only place they live, I'm thinking, *the only spot in the world, in their little herd, on this little island, and here they are calm as heaven, chewing and looking at us.* They are the only ones, ringed in by danger, and yet they're intent on what they're doing, only mildly curious about us, as if nothing were more assured than the fact of their ongoingness.

And suddenly I can hardly bear to look at him, this dark-eyed fellow, because I can't see his beauty; I can't see anything but his disappearance.

It's almost exactly three years, this night in the Keys, since my partner Wally's death. He and I were together for nearly a dozen years; the last five of those we lived under the shadow of his diagnosis as HIV positive, and then in the darkness of his AIDS diagnosis. We had time to prepare; we made sure the last of his life held as much brightness as we could muster, although it was a terrifying confrontation with an implacable process of erasure. One of the things erased was our sense of a shared future; we'd been together long enough to have become part of one another's lives, involved in one another's memories, each a part of the way the other saw the world. Over a dozen years our relationship had changed, as any marriage does; we'd grown more companionable, less passionate, more understanding of one another, our partnership strong enough to allow elasticity, openness, strength. I don't know—can't know—what would have become of us had Wally lived, except that I'm certain he would always have been a presence in my life; one of the things we lost, in his dying, was the continuing adventure of our history together. The ways we would have evolved and changed died with him.

Fourteen months later, I became involved with Paul. I'd known him for years, as a fellow writer, a friend in the neighborhood, someone who helped out by looking in on Wally when I was away. I'd always liked him and never imagined us as lovers, though in retrospect I can see that I always *did* brighten when he entered a room. This is a first for me, this experience of friendship shifting to romance—I suppose like many gay men I'd been inclined to sex first, then seeing what happened from there. With Paul it was entirely different; I felt comfortable with him, I felt known, and it seemed crucial to me that he had known Wally, too—so that my past had a reality for him, not a reported, imagined territory but something witnessed. All this sounds very rational, and indeed I did think these things, but the fact is that what I felt was an overwhelming, swelling tide of lust—a veritable Bay of Fundy inrush of desire that seemed to quite sweep reason away. What was I doing? I didn't know, but my body did.

After loss, the head and heart may say, *I'm tired, it's use-*

less, I can't continue, what can there be to treasure when every-thing gets taken away? But that's where desire comes in. The blessedly reliable body says *I want.* Food, sex, a mas-sage, a hot bath, it almost doesn't matter what; the plain fact of wanting implies continuance, persistence. Often, during that first year of grief, my sadness would over-whelm my desire; I'd want, say, the comfort and distrac-tion of touch only to find that I couldn't focus my atten-tion in the present. *Trying* to desire is usually disastrous, of course, merely a willful exercise. The real thing rises from somewhere beneath the will, though it helps if the will cooperates.

With Paul, there was no element of trying; suddenly I found myself enthralled with this lovely man's body, a body I could attend to because I trusted him so much, felt at ease with him. When we began this new phase of our relationship, I was forty-one and he thirty-five. Af-ter a dozen years of domestic life, I'd forgotten about the state of sexual intoxication, that drunken feeling of be-ing caught up in the body of another, enraptured. Oh, Wally and I had sex until fairly late in his life. We weren't exclusively monogamous, and it wasn't as if I'd forgotten about erotic pleasure. But married sex (which tends to-ward the warm and pleasant) and casual sex (which is often about as intense as a nice lunch) are not the same thing as the dizzy thrall of a new sexual obsession. I hadn't imagined that such a thing would happen to me again—and I didn't miss it, exactly; it just didn't occur to me. But now I loved it, I was at sea in it, despite the fact that I hated the way it had come to me, that I would gladly have traded passion for my old married life, if the world worked that way, if it made any difference at all what we would exchange for what we had lost.

I was very happy, which confused the hell out of me. I liked this new intensity, these deep pleasures my new life yielded, and yet at the same time I found myself divided, half of my gaze turned towards the past. A sort of negotiation seemed to be taking place between then and now, between what I'd had and what the world offered this moment, between who I'd been and who I was becoming. Much of this went on, I think, on a semiconscious level. Sometimes with Paul I believe I'd simply drift away someplace, not quite at home in my body or our bed.

Perhaps falling in love again must always be a complicated dance of loyalties. A dead man resides in my head, and a live one lives in my house—our house now—and I am not aware that I am being loyal to one or the other until something trips me up. Sometimes, for instance, I notice in my own speech a locution which isn't really mine, but rather a phrase or accent of Wally's. I never know I am about to sound like him until the words tumble out of my mouth—sometimes just some bit of nonsense he was fond of like "Hi, sly guy." When I would begin a sentence with "surely," as in "Surely you jest," Wally would invariably say, "*Don't* call me Shirley." Now this comes off my own tongue when I least expect it, and I've caught myself feeling—well, odd. This man is in my language, my thinking, my pleasures, my way of seeing—which is what happens when you're together a dozen years, no, fifteen, save that for three of those years he has been dead.

Then there are those pleasures that belong to the new relationship. Going to visit my parents, with whom I have a complex and somewhat fraught relationship, I told Paul how I felt and realized that he understood exactly—which Wally, with his big, happy family, never really did. Paul and I love lots of the same books, admire many of the same artists, share passions that Wally and I did not. Of course, I think, different men, different experiences. But I've also thought, *Oh, I'm enjoying something with Paul that Wally couldn't enjoy.* I've wondered, guiltily, if I liked my new relationship better.

Which would be a betrayal, wouldn't it?

This business of loyalty and of comparison is invidious, both stupid and pointless, and yet it seems an unavoidable aspect of loving again. If I love Paul, will I lose Wally again? Do I deny him by moving on? Is loving the present relinquishing the past? Such questions are the painful stuff of a process of adjustment, of reconsideration, of change.

I understand this, but it doesn't make it easier. Paul has been a workaday saint of patience. He somehow manages to communicate to me that whatever I am feeling is all right, that he accepts what I'm struggling with, and that such confusion isn't surprising. He's simply said that he cannot know what I feel, though he empathizes and tries to imagine, and when he does he finds it overwhelming—so how could I not be overwhelmed? He's been startled when people have asked if it bothers him that I've written about Wally and me, or when I read from that work; he's always quietly polite about it, though I know in his head he's quoting the downtown drag queen, The Lady Bunny: "It's the Nineties, honey." What gay man now, he reasons, doesn't deal with loss upon loss? He knows that Wally was a sweetheart, that we had a good life, and that this history has nothing to do with him, save that it enlarges me. Don't we want our lovers deepened and educated by experience?

But I feel, if anything, too well schooled, my capacity for joy tarnished. It shows up in little ways. Setting up housekeeping together, I get so tired that I wonder if I can possibly get it together to pick out towels or napkins; aren't I too old for this? Meaning, of course, not in years but in attitude. Aren't the domestic trappings, the daily ephemera, an elaborate defense against the void, a set of frills placed in opposition to the ineluctable fact of death?

But I know that I love Paul too much to simply go off somewhere and lick the gaping wound in me—the crack in my faith in life—and wait for it to heal. The smoke and rapture of the sexual thrall isn't exactly gone, but it's cleared enough for me to see what a good soul he is, how perceptive and how generous, and how deeply and clearly he sees me. In short, he's too good to pass up, and the fact is that hearts probably don't heal through a rest cure anyway. You put the muscle to use again, and in that fashion it will be strengthened.

I have tried to be patient with myself, as Paul has been

patient with me, and indeed my own face seems to me less shadowed by the weight of the past. I've made progress, or I think I have. But here I am, idling in the humid dark of a Florida highway, almost unable to look at this little deer because I'm afraid he's going to die.

To acknowledge reality is to admit vulnerability. And if you steel yourself to that, what happens is that ultimately you don't feel much of anything. The apertures of perception have to narrow, as they try to select those aspects of the world which seem benign. And so it was that the reality of that diminutive herd—*only here, on this island, nowhere for them to go, grazing on the side of the highway, in all the world they're the only ones of their kind*—seemed to enter into my awareness a little at a time, after the fact, over the course of days: the delicate legs and hooves in the long grass, the clear and unflinching gaze, the elegant clutch of horns like a crown, the triumphant flourish at the end of a concerto.

LAST NIGHT a man from Boston, a stranger, called me because his lover had just been diagnosed with PML (Progressive Multifocal Leukoencephalopathy, a rare neurological disease that affects 3 to 4 percent of AIDS patients). He'd read *Heaven's Coast*, a memoir I'd written about my experience of grief, so he knew that Wally had died of the same condition. I didn't pick up the answering machine when he called—a self-protective habit, since I don't always want to be at the mercy of the phone and Paul and I were just about to sit down to dinner. I'd made a big salad, and we'd lit the candles in the chandelier in what's now a dining room again, after the emergency rearrangement of the house around Wally's needs, which lasted three years; it's wonderful to have the house back in what seems its natural order, with a dining table under its five-candled black iron chandelier hanging from the ceiling's hemlock beams, and the living room not a hospital room anymore. Deprived of the big bed which filled and anchored (and basically swallowed) the room all that time, our dogs Arden and Beau lie on the old wool Indian rug I rescued from a burned house in Des Moines nearly twenty years ago.

So we sat down to the blue table, the white salad bowl gleaming in the candlelight, but all I could really feel was dread, thinking of that poor voice working to stay calm on the machine, looking for information and through it either hope or solace or at least the consoling sense of something to *do*. It horrifies me, fills me with sorrow, the prospect of another couple at the beginning of that long passage. They can't know what they're about to enter. I eat the dinner I've been so hungry for but I'm not really taking pleasure in it. When we're finished I call the man back.

Grief is very like a bad back: What you have to do, in order to function, is basically forget that you hurt. Then the limitations, the discomfort start to normalize, to seem like the everyday condition of being; after a while you aren't even aware that you're hobbling, or holding yourself carefully in order not to go into spasms of pain. I have lived in grief so long I don't see it. I forget that it has constricted my breathing so that my lungs don't hold what they used to. I forget that I use a hundred subterfuges not to feel what I feel, sly little distractions of work, busyness, activities that are necessary but don't have to be pursued with the obliterating single-mindedness I sometimes practice, a focus designed solely to hold pain at bay. Grief's daily habit is constriction; it holds back spontaneity, it curtails response to experience, because you never know when the spontaneous reaction to some bit of stimulus the world offers is going to be devastation. Here I sit at my desk, cluttered as desks are with little things which are the amulets or talismans which surround the alchemical process of writing. These things are laden with meaning, always. In my case they are: a pin of filigreed silvery metal, eye shaped, set with eight glass gems of a faceted blue deep as an Arizona sky in June, arranged in a field of tiny gems of a lighter sapphire. My friend Lynda used to wear it on her black beret, or on a coat lapel, before the car accident that killed her. And here's a perfectly smooth "stone," of frosted black glass, a paperweight Bobby stole from one of the stores where he worked, long ago when he still *could* work. And, dominating the field, a lamb, made of painted cement, with glass eyes glued on, the skewed innocence of its expression lending it the look of Blake's emblems of innocence; it is a jaunty, artless lamb. One steamy summer day in Vermont, Wally and I carried it home from the Dog River Sale Barn, a commodious cathedral of a building stuffed with old musical instruments and ugly Victorian furniture. The lamb was the one thing there I loved. We drove the dirt road along the river, through rich bottomland gardens of lettuces and flowers, squash and rhubarb that some truck farmer would carry in to the farmers' market in Montpelier, the lazy little river and the green squares of produce all buzzing and humming with promise. Now the lamb guards a cherrybark canister in which I keep a handful of Wally's ashes.

I want to live with these things, but in order to do so I close myself to their power. Yet my heart opens when I don't expect it, when I have finished distracting myself, and these things are suddenly vessels of grief, tokens of the weight I carry through the world. Memory seems like some huge, clumsy scaffolding I have to wear, a clanking apparatus to which I've become attached. How can I find the strength to carry all this? And what is the alternative—erasure? A tabula rasa? Neither desirable nor possible.

John's grateful that I've called him back. He has the orderly and calm approach of a man who's working hard, expending incredible energy to stay focused on what needs to be done, to hold on to what he can hope for. Kevin's illness is taking a very different course from Wally's. HIV positive and healthy for eleven years, he experienced a sudden drop in his T cells two months ago. He began taking antivirals and the new protease inhibitors, and went ahead with plans to begin a new job. Everything seemed fine till the first day of work, when he was asked to fill out a W-4 form and suddenly found he couldn't write. He could understand whatever was said to him perfectly well, but when he tried to respond he couldn't find the word for, say, pencil, or book. What, John wants to know, should he expect?

I hear in what he asks, of course, my own questions, years ago, when I so much needed someone to tell me what was going on, what to expect. It seems that John's gotten more hope than I did (there have been, according to Kevin's neurologist, some cases of spontaneous remission), but not much in the way of prognosis. Will it get worse? When? I give what little information I have, encouraging John to get his resources lined up now, to find out about the help he's going to need, since it's possible that Kevin's condition could change very quickly. It isn't much. I let John talk about how well they've been doing—their suddenly quashed plans to adopt, their professional lives, their involvement in taking care of Kevin's elderly parents, which seems a kind of dark rehearsal—and I can tell he's glad for the chance to talk. I suppose there is some use in my simply saying, "This must be devastating for you."

But it makes me feel hopeless, this conversation, as if I had more strength back when I was struggling with Wally's illness and even in the shattered time when I was planting one foot in front of the other in the months after his death. Was it that I so desperately needed hope in order to continue that I was given some, or that I wrested it out of experience and perception?

Later—the apparent crisis passed, my life moving on—there seemed to settle around me this brooding atmosphere. Were an engraver to represent me I'd be covered with a web of crosshatching, little darkening lines creating a shadowed zone. Things penetrate through the shadow but they don't lift it, at least for very long. The good dinner we've made, the candlelight are gestures too flimsy to hold back the swell of sorrow, the still palpable fear.

Though there are things so bright that, even through the darkening filter my gaze places over experience, they shine: my golden retriever Beau asleep on the floor beside my desk, his long body fit between a stack of papers and an open doorway, his paws twitching rhythmically as he dreams. Paul's gaze in the sidewalk cafe where we ate dinner yesterday, expectant, full of interest in the future. (Their brightness makes me think, Am I being unfair to him, only partly available, when he seems available to be all the way? Is it fair to involve my life with his when I am still in this state of damage? Is this me, this limping thing, from here on out?)

This morning the four of us—Paul and Beau and Arden and I—all lay together on the beach at Herring Cove. It was a foggy morning, no visible dividing line between sea and sky, just one barely rippling continuum of gray still enough to reveal, in the middle distance, the playful black fins of fish breaking surface a dozen yards from shore. The sea seemed almost completely still, but one wave broke all the way along the shoreline, continuous, like a zipper being opened the whole length of the cove, then starting over again. When we sprawled on the sand I closed my eyes and became filled by the rush and splash of that sound. In the gaps between waves, the higher, delicate pitch of the foghorn at Race Point seemed to open right in the center of my forehead. Clear note of the horn, then lap and encompassing susurration of the waves: I felt myself letting go, dissolving, at ease. I'm tired of carrying my own weight. All I want to do is rest in the palms of that sound, in the laving and buoying waters, and be lifted by them.

I TRIED—I struggled mightily—not to hate life because it had death in it. I was sick and tired of grief, which is tantamount to saying that I was sick of myself. Weary of my own whining, my constant effort to negotiate with the past, keeping it in its place or letting it into the present in measured amounts. I was exhausted with trying to see what was good in grief, what could be learned from it, how loss enriched my perceptions or my spirit. To hell with that; I'd struggled to see something redemptive in the experience because I *had* to; I was dog-tired of that particular kind of work.

Though I *had* been educated by grief; I had seen a man I loved die radiantly, almost heroically; I'd seen his freedom, and transformation, as the life left him and leapt to join the invisible. I'd seen, in those raw winter days after his death, into the frozen animal heart of the world, through which the flesh carries us. I learned how the God in us moves over the body's still water when we die. I learned not to be afraid of dying; I learned to believe that wherever and whatever he was now, Wally was fine.

But try as I would, *I* was not fine. I tried to focus on how much I had been given—the gifts and privileges which had come to me, in these dark years, at a time when I most needed bolstering. And it wasn't as if I walked around weeping all the time; I found sources of pleasure in love and work, in beauty and in play. But I was nagged by the feeling that beneath those pleasures lay this wound, an absence which seemed to function the way astronomers say black holes do, sucking light into itself, canceling out other possibilities—so in spite of being loved, in spite of being offered hopes and possibilities, I still somehow felt withered and dark and small, a dried and twisted little root of a thing, without vitality or heart.

What was the matter with me? I had a new man who was not only crazy about me but absolutely patient, willing to wait out my storms of grief, my moods of unavailability, my darker hours—and he was sexy and passionate about life and eager for things, as if in our love the world seemed to be beginning for him all over again. And that was part of the trouble: *he* was raring to start a life, fresh for the tumultuous change and tumble that begins in the simple act of finding someone you really like and ends up transforming the heart, pulling you to places you never thought you'd go—the way, as my friend Richard puts it, love translates itself into *adventure*, not just a feeling but the making of a life.

But I had made a life. And though I wanted to begin again, I found myself in love and in grief simultaneously, which is no easy place to be. I wanted to be energetic again, as ebullient about the world as Paul (was I, once?) but much of the time I felt numbed, going through the motions, though not exactly in grief, which seems to me something sharper and more focused. What I was in was despair, the walls of which were, in their own strange way, higher; grief referred to a specific object, a specific loss. And while I certainly had that, and felt each day's portion of that loss doled out to me, chewed, swallowed, and accepted, something else had occurred, too. I had generalized from grief towards the nature of things. How could I love in a world whose salient characteristic was relentless erasure?

THE Japanese Tea Garden, Golden Gate Park, San Francisco: an early afternoon sheened with silvery coastal light. A mother-of-pearl layer of cloud thinned to a high glaze by sun, then the atmosphere darkens to something softer, the muffling intimacy of rain.

I'm thinking of the world in layers, a meditation provoked by the koi: beneath the surface of the absolutely clear ponds that thread through this garden, these calm presences drift and angle. They seem to float without effort, though now and then a purposeful flick of the two translucent fins on either side of the body propels them forward. Who was the Japanese philosopher who said, "A fish never makes an aesthetic mistake"? These big, lovely fellows are the confident princes of another world, gleaming in their supple chain mail. Just when I round a curve in the path or come up over a little rise,

another's revealed, the garden's secret jewels: here a
speckled opal, here a blazing orangey-gold "like shook
foil." Here's the most startling of all: a pale chiffon yellow, its vibrant intensity amplified by the gray light of
the day. He turns on his side as he swims, as if to scratch
his lemon flanks on the pond bottom, flashing to heaven
a belly of birthday-candle yellow, a shimmery lemon
meringue. He makes me catch my breath; what in all the
world glows like that? And his happy, doglike rolling
and scratching—who'd have thought a fish so capable of
evidencing pleasure?

These koi move beneath a complicated surface—
even, occasionally, break through that horizontal scrim
which is busy giving back the dull sheen of the sky and
the bulk of trees, reflections even of individual leaves, as
well as the interruption of actual leaves floating on the
water. And, as if the surface didn't already have enough
work to do, it's begun to rain a little, so that the drops of
rain send out spreading rings which shiver all the other
reflections and overlap with other circles. The black-
and-silver skin of the pond becomes a kind of dreamy
geometry lesson, demonstration of an indecipherable
mathematics.

I wouldn't think so much about the third layer, above
water and surface, save that it is threaded now by birds—
sleek black citizens whose predominant feature, besides
their elegant necks, always in motion, are the shiny little
black beads of their eyes, which are vivid pinpoints of
subjectivity—places where the air seems to look out at
itself, at us all. Strange to think of so many vantage
points, the air full of locations: points of departure, per-

spectives, places to stand, intentions. These feathered stances pulse and hurry, pause and cock their heads, shift back and forth on wire legs, turn those glamorous necks every which way.

And there is, too, a pair of blue jays, their Virgin-of-Guadalupe azure almost impossibly bright in the rain, a cobalt leap and flutter from branch to stone lantern to boulder to branch, in some kind of chattering and gesticulating dialogue with each other, two quick blue thoughts circling around and around in the air. (They are actually multiple shades of blue, each hue seeming to vibrate at a different speed, a subtly shifting degree of intensity, which is why, in flight, they seem like visible music, a chromatic range in shifting relation to one another, a theme with variations. One of the hues is exactly the color of an old painted door in my house in Provincetown, the color antique dealers call "old blue.") One goes down to the water's edge and jumps in, splashing its wings rapidly to beat the water into a tumble of droplets in the air, commingling the three layers of things I've been watching into one. Is it me who has made the separation? Obviously the boundaries between air and water are permeable ones—the koi break the surface to feed and splash, the rain and leaves raddle the reflective skim, the birds leave off throwing their darting reflections on the water in order to enter into it and worry the surface further. Water is the physical demonstration of responsiveness; nothing is more immediately and visibly reactive. Water plays back for us every force affecting it, every nuance, every bit of life.

Today it seems to me that time has just the layered

quality of this garden. I've come here in a taxi, essentially by mistake, since I'd planned to go to the Museum of Asian Art. Tired of talking (I am on a book tour, a round of readings and interviews which require me to try to articulate again, in a different arena, what I've already written about love and grief), I wanted the silence and poise of Japanese ceramics or Chinese scrolls. But almost as soon as the taxi's pulled away, I realize the museum's closed; the sign on the door tells me I've come on the wrong day. I turn from the door to the round ornamental pool in front of the museum, and realize first that the turtle sitting on a lip of stone protruding from the water is not bronze but alive, and then that I have seen this before—have, in fact, *done* this before. In 1989, on a vacation in San Francisco, Wally and I did exactly the same thing, arriving at the museum doors on a Monday or Tuesday, and happily watching a turtle—*this* turtle?—among the water lilies in the ornamental pool. And then we wandered next door, to the Japanese Tea Garden. So the warm fragrance of brewing tea coming toward me from the sheltered area where people are sitting with teapots and rice crackers takes me back to that day, those flavors: seven years passed, same mistake, same pleasures. And new ones, since the garden seems engineered to ensure that we notice the complicated matrix of this particular day. New sadness, as well. I feel rather like that blue jay, mixing up the layers of time till they're indistinguishable.

Though, in fact, the scent of the tea—more present, in the rainy air—does not bring back the past as much as I would like it to. I hope that some particularly vivid, buried memory of Wally, of an hour together, will come back to me here. But it doesn't; I'm more aware of the irony—here we were, here I am—than of any vivid sense of him. Memory of this kind can't be willed; if it isn't the time for it, then it isn't. But I am wishing for such an encounter with the past because my relationship with the past is in a state of confusion.

Always a complicated dynamic, it's been spun around of late by this tour, by reading to audiences about Wally and his death, by talking to journalists and interviewers about grief. I am no longer in the habit of talking about him every day; I talk *to* him nearly daily, but it's an interior conversation, and I am not accustomed to all this bringing of memory out into the outer world. This brings him closer, particularly when I am reading to audiences for whom I know the epidemic is a pressing reality. Their faces remind me that these words have the force of actuality for them; they're here because it is important for them to find their experience mirrored in language. And writing is only capable of that when it is crafted and honed—not just the expressive journal entry in which the writer's feelings are paramount, but the shapely work which also allows the *reader* to feel.

But therein lies a paradox: these words both evoke the past and hold it at a distance. As I read them to audiences, I sometimes re-experience the past but I always re-experience my own language, as if my words were gradually taking the place of my memory, covering the past over with bits of phrases—like a sort of elaborate mosaic pavement, something from the basilica of San Marco in Venice, assembled over the surface of my memory—so that it *becomes* a surface, a made replacement for the felt thing.

One night, not long before the visit to the garden, I had an awful paroxysm of doubt, a terror that by repeating my story, by turning my life with Wally into art, I had made it *more* difficult for me to remember him. In the act of making him memorable to others, had I removed him from myself? Had I only intensified or exacerbated my loss? Or worse, done some disservice to him, made him smaller? I don't want my story, the artifact of memory, but something less pure, less selected: the unpredictability, the otherness, of another being.

And this is another way the dead die to us. They are not there to correct our impressions, to keep us from getting too confident in our understandings of them. The living will always make sure that we can't fool ourselves into thinking we totally know them; something will always confound our perceptions, challenge our certainty. But of the dead, we know what we know, and over time our memories and the narrative we make of them begin to seem fixed, not subject to revision by experience.

What I was feeling was, finally, simple, familiar. I missed him. All the stories I'd made to represent him, all the writing I've done to capture something of us, are at last doomed to fail; nothing is captured, nothing is held, because no matter what gesture we make to render the world, no matter how seemingly large and encompassing the gesture is, the world resists. The world is larger than art. "The world is wily," Susan Mitchell says in one of her poems, "and doesn't want to be caught." My poetry and my prose sometimes seem to me a complicated set of negotiations with death, of attempted accommodations to mortality: *Here is a way to think of dying which might be bearable, which might be something close to all right.* And yet it's not acceptable, not all right, though one cannot stop making the negotiations, cannot stop the proposals of possibility, in spite of the fact that death will knock the papers from the table, will end all discussions, will break off talks without hope of resolution.

In the landscape of the garden, I locate myself not with the splendid yellow fish or the quick aerial cogitation of the jays; it's that calm but nonetheless never-still surface of the water with which I identify. I am trembled by wind, written upon by the sky and all its passages of cloud and of wings. I am fluid in time as well as in space; it's foolish of me to wish to recapture the past, because I *am* the past, what there is of it; it's entirely entwined in my subjectivity. I carry it. And I am now, as well, inscribed by every passing force, unstable, rain marked, clear.

I don't have the experience I might wish for, of vivid memory, the past recaptured. Wally and I are not here. But I am, and more to the point the garden *is*: this matrix of levels, this common flesh in its multiple forms, these winged and finned thoughts and surfaces upon which the forces of the world meet. I am happy here, seeing all this life, implicated in it, even if my grief is useless, even if my longing and my work have come to nothing.

Not redemption, not reclamation. But perhaps not nothing. I am thinking of a chilling statement of Yeats's: "All that is personal soon rots unless it is packed in ice or salt." He meant the preservative chill and saline of form, the poet's icy verbal brine which might pickle poor mortal forms caught in time. I've quoted it to students a thousand times, but suddenly I think he's wrong; all that is personal rots *anyway*; it's the ice and salt that last. All the particulars of love and desire and memory and doubt poured into poetry vanish, as the poem becomes, in time, a vessel for the reader's feeling, the writer's distinctive individual experience faded away. The form lasts long beyond the life it was made to hold.

And even the preservative container will vanish, when no one can read that language anymore, or the books that contained it fall to pieces. Think of Sappho's poems torn to shreds in Egypt to wrap the mummy of a crocodile, and the little strips of paper come to light a century ago which display just the shards. Stays against time are temporary; our attempts to hold time at bay, of course, are made inside of time, exist within in it, as everything does. The shreds survive, and then nothing.

And yet the flux, the moment, the participation in the life of the world, in that shimmered and inscribed surface, erased and rewritten, scribbled and trembled and reconfigured—isn't that something more than nothing? What could we ever be but the flux, the liquid page written by this day, right now, in which is involved all the past there is, as well as all tomorrows?

Not nothing. A man comes up to me at a book signing, and asks me to sign his book. "I'm Mark," he says. "Would you sign this for Jim and Mark?" It turns out Jim's been dead a month. Mark's face is open and radiant, that look that people have when the world has cracked open in front of them, when they themselves have cracked. He could burst into tears at any moment, or sing, or praise something. "I'm a Buddhist," he says. I think he wants me to know this because it's meant to tell me he's all right, that he can stand at some distance from attachment, from life and death, that he doesn't believe that Jim has ended exactly, because was "Jim" there in the first place? At least I think that's what he means; "I'm a Buddhist" seems like complicated shorthand.

Then he tells me that someone read a passage from *Heaven's Coast* at Jim's memorial service; the book hasn't been out long, and it seems extraordinary that people are *using* it, that the book is already involved, independently of me, implicated in lives (and deaths). And then I realize I don't care if what I make lasts for fifteen minutes or fifteen years or (imagine!) fifteen centuries; it makes no difference at all. It isn't the preservative part of art that matters; it's the *use.* It's the word that works as water-surface, mirroring back human life and feeling; it's the act of writing and reading which extends the small size of my humanity in the direction of others. I am allowed to keep neither Wally nor anything else, but in fact I am allowed to give him, or a version of him, away. I cannot even keep myself, but I can give the word that's written by the world on the surface of myself away. To be spoken by Mark, for Jim; to be spoken by that

Mark for himself; to be written by this Mark for that one; to be said on the air, as it is written on air, by my hand of air, out of my history of breathing.

Not nothing, not yet. There's some faith in art I have that won't quite leave me. Maybe we can't get the world just right, can't get it captured in language, but it seems to be possible to suggest enough of the way the clear bright skin of the pond shines. A version of the world— my work, what there is before me to be done—which could exist between us, not exactly capturing the un-capturable past but indicating, somehow, through the agencies of art, enough of that complexly wavering sur-face, enough of the skin of the world, that you might see beneath it the mystery: the pale-side-of-lemon-peel fish swims and shines, turning first to one side and then the other, rolling, himself liquid, a big pale treasure, alive.

For weeks now, Paul has been casually working on a song. He has a sort of semisecret life as a composer of liturgical music; his settings of psalms show up in hym-nals and songbooks all over the country. I didn't know this about him at first; he screens his avocation behind his more public identity as a writer. What a delicious identity to keep in the closet!

The song has been coming in little snatches he hums and sings when he's vacuuming or otherwise occupied, but today he seems to have composed enough of it in his head to be ready to move to his electronic keyboard. He's at the dining table with the instrument and staff pa-

per for noting down the arrangement, a translation of
the Psalms open beside him. The one he's setting is
number 137, and he's playing the opening bars again and
again, with slight variations:

> *Beside the streams of Babylon,*
> *We sat down and we wept,*
> *When Zion's memory came to mind*
> *We sat down and we wept—*

He doesn't know that I have come into the next room.
He is shy about playing and singing in front of me,
which seems odd, given how much time we spend together, and oddly touching. I am watching from the
doorway. I love the way he hunches forward, as if he's
fitting his lanky frame around the keyboard; because
I'm watching from behind, I can see the play of muscle
in his neck as he mouths the words. I love the slightly
tinny sound the keys make when struck—like a badly
recorded harpsichord—and the sunlight through the
old lace in the east-facing windows, his soft voice working out the details and harmonies in this rather cheerful
song of exile.

I am, myself, in a strange land, and I don't know the
harmonies here yet. How could I? And yet the song
seems entirely full of promise; the melody seems to say
that if exile will not end, it will be accepted, there will
be terms for it. My lover has that concentration, that ab-
sorption in the moment, in which it's impossible not to
see his handsomeness, his—how to say it?—his presence as himself, both self-forgetful and completely in-

volved. It draws everyone around him into the present, too.

Including the dogs, who are lying at his feet as if they like the chime of the keys, the subtle variations of the repeated phrases. Arden has his head on his paws. As the tune continues, Beau leans back, as if the song were entering into him, and then begins to roll on his back, as if the music and Paul's voice and the warm sunlight through the lace curtains were playing all along the length of his spine. He is the same color as the light through the lace. So much pleasure, in this constellation of things: warmth and sun and the sweet configuration of voice and music. It's as if Beau can't contain his happiness; it wells up and requires him to move. Soon Paul will notice that I am here, watching, and, though he'll be happy to see me, I'll also break the moment's domestic spell, this little bright instance of what I love, which I am grateful now to stand and watch, unseen.

For Better or Worse

MY WEDDING was the simplest of affairs. I was married in a lawyer's office in midtown Manhattan, my only concession to bridely behaviour a bunch of white roses tied with white satin ribbon. A judge said some apposite words, the groom screwed up his face and cried, I clutched the roses and felt a ninny. Afterwards, we lunched with our two witnesses—my brother and a friend—at the Four Seasons. In toasting me, my brother said, "To my sister, whom I have seen through thick and thin. This is the thickest." Then we went back to work.

This description does not convey how special the day was. Sometimes when things are planned least, they turn out best. First, the weather. Sodden for weeks, it unexpectedly cleared, and we had sky so blue and air so fresh people could be seen standing still, noses a-twitch, like rabbits in spring. Next, the judge. We had expected him to be perfunctory, but he surprised us with his sincerity. He talked of seriousness of purpose, courage, resolve, effort—to my mind exactly what was going to be needed. The judge, we like to think, spoke from his heart.

My female coworkers, who could spend a year planning a wedding, were shocked at my casual attitude. They urged me to buy a new dress, preferably in cream or white, and I told them I had a perfectly good one, navy in colour, at home in my closet. Couldn't we come up with something more romantic than a lawyer's office? they asked, and I put on the face of a cynic and informed them it was an appropriate place for a transaction largely legal in nature. They felt insulted, so it was as a propitiatory gesture to every woman who has donned tulle and crossed her fingers that I bought the roses.

When the English feminist Dora Russell married the philosopher Bertrand Russell, her only concession to bridely behaviour was a bunch of sweet peas wrapped in newspaper. Dora took a dim view of marriage, and with good reason: in those days a wife was the property of her husband. But Bertie, much older and more conservative than Dora, was eager to tie the knot. Also a child was on the way. She took the line of least resistance.

She regretted everything, even the sweet peas. The marriage ended twelve years later, the bitterest of lawsuits and the hardest of feelings all around, with Dora getting, as she had feared, the short end of the patriarchal stick. She blamed a system weighted toward men, but also herself for betraying her beliefs in the first place.

As an outspoken critic of marriage, she had been hypocritical in entering into one. More than that: She had gone against the grain of her being. Dora wrote in a letter, "I shall certainly never quite recover from the feeling of disgrace I had in marrying."

The laws relating to divorce, while far from perfect, have improved since Dora's day, but I felt uncomfortable aligning myself with an institution that hasn't served women well. Ironically, because participants in long-term relationships have no legal protection in the United States, I found that I had more to gain if I married. Still, I ran around in my twenties with a motorcycle helmet stickered with the slogan, "Better Dead Than Wed"; my marriage was a noticeable about-face. What had happened to my fight and fire? Was I turning into rice pudding?

If I have learned anything from my years as a feminist, it is that there are no oughts and shoulds, blacks and whites. The truth is, like Dora Russell, I was taking the path of least resistance; I could have lived with my husband, Bob, without marrying him if the principle had been important. But I had prospered in the relationship. Bob is the most interesting man I have ever met; I might not always like him, but he never bores me. His support is absolute. And he does all the cooking. I would do a lot for him, even marry.

Bob wanted the security. Contrary to popular belief, men are much keener on "wedded bliss" than women; studies show they go to pieces without a partner while women thrive. I have noticed that since the marriage, arguments calling for a divorce by sundown notwith-standing, Bob has been more at ease. As for myself, al-though those twin phrases of possessiveness, "my hus-band" and "my wife," still set me on edge, I also have the feeling of coming into a safe harbour.

The act of marrying was significant for another rea-son: It focused me on the future. I needed to be clear about my intentions because Bob is twenty-five years older than I am. In fact, the year we were married he turned sixty-five. A senior citizen, no less. I would be promising to do my best to stay with him not for a story-book "forever" but as he grows old.

Some background. We met seven years ago. Bob had given up a career as an art director to paint, but he and his wife were embezzled by their business manager. The strain caused the marriage, his second, to break up, and Bob, stony broke, had to go back to work. He took a job redesigning a magazine where I was the managing edi-tor. We had coffee one day to discuss the redesign. Im-pulsively, I brought up the subject of poetry. This was risky: a penchant for poetry is best kept under wraps in the halls of commerce lest one be thought unreliable. As it turned out, Bob was receptive. We became friends.

Bob wasn't my type—he was too old and too nice and too available. I was the sort of person who specialised in despair. I took as my role models women who loved his-trionically: Sylvia Plath, Anna Kavan, Jean Rhys. But circumstances were forcing me to question my past be-haviour. I discovered I had things to learn from a man who had started over again at an age when most people would turn their faces to the wall.

Occasionally we play the "if only we had met earlier" game, but the truth is we are together only because we met as late as we did. At any earlier time, Bob would not have been interested in someone as prickly as I, someone who couldn't massage a male ego if her life depended on it, nor I in a veteran of two marriages which, by his account, were pre-Copernican, with everything revolving around him.

I wanted, of course, a relationship in which neither of us would dominate. Easier said than done. When I think of the dynamics of our marriage, sumo wrestling comes to mind. There we are, knees bent, facing each other. I am wiry but tough, good at defending my ground, but Bob has muscle that I don't. It comes from sixty-odd years of asserting his will and not doubting himself at every turn. Of being a man, in short.

Even the most enlightened of men bring to marriage the advantage that automatically accrues to them in our culture. As Phyllis Rose writes in her book *Parallel Lives*, they are playing with the wind behind them:

Women who are sensitive to power negotiations in their relationships . . . may prefer men with some handicap . . . the absence of one of those surpluses, or advantages over women with which men are traditionally expected to enter marriage—height, money, age, social status, achievement.

Ironically, the embezzlement made our relationship possible.

Anyone thinking of marrying someone considerably older than themselves can't avoid doing a little arithmetic. One woman told me she did hers aloud to her husband-to-be. "When I'm forty, you'll be sixty, when

I'm fifty"—rising panic—"you'll be seventy, when I'm sixty you'll be"—complete panic—"dead." "What makes you think I'll die before you do?" he asked.

On hearing of my plans to marry, people went out of their way to tell me stories of "May-December" relationships where, after a few good years, the women become caretakers of invalids. Others pointed out that anyone can be laid low by ill health. True enough. A woman I know married a man her own age when she was in her thirties, only to have him stricken by a fatal degenerative disease. "You promise to marry for better or worse," she said, "but you never understand how worse worse can be."

All the same, the likelihood of marriage being for worse rather than better increases with age. We might not be eager to acknowledge the possibility of chronic illness, dwindling energy, and death, but insurance companies are, as their actuarial tables demonstrate. I cannot say that I have made my peace with this, although I am trying not to worry unduly. Seize the day, seize the hour, as Chairman Mao said. I do notice that I am reading the obituary page, something I never did before, mentally cheering those who make it into their eighties and beyond, tsk-tsk-ing those with more modest innings.

I have had little experience with illness, so when Bob got the flu a few months back and was forced to take naps in the middle of the day, I was horrified to discover how unsympathetic I was. I was beside myself with impatience. I would shake him awake, saying, "Time to get up. You've slept long enough." Of course, what I really meant was, "Don't get sick on me. And now I've found you, don't die on me."

I talked about my marriage with a friend who is in her sixties. I hadn't known that her husband, who keeps to a gruelling work schedule, is more than a decade older than she. This was the first year, she told me, that she had noticed any difference in their ages. The example: They left a party early because he was tired.

"How old exactly is Sam?" I asked.

"Eighty."

I started to laugh. Eighty and this is the first year she has noticed! So much for my fears.

"You know," I confided, "sometimes Bob cups his hand behind his ear and I think, Oh my goodness, my grandfather!"

She pulled a wry face; she has had the same experience. In a more serious vein, we both agreed that our husbands are extraordinarily supportive. With age, the need in them to be cock of the walk has diminished.

Not all women think older men are such finds. I swapped life stories with a woman on a plane whose husband had left her high and dry as soon as the kids were grown. Within a year of his departure, she had started her own firm and was doing very well, thank you. She had also taken up with a man half her age. "I don't want a man my age," she said. "They're too rigid. I want a youngie!" Youngie? Nauseating term. But it was heartening to hear a woman boldly stating her preferences. Choosing instead of being chosen.

As for marriage, she told me she wouldn't touch it with fire tongs. I don't blame her. It is a job of work. And rhetoric about partnership aside—"A deceptively lucid ideal" writes Phyllis Rose—there is something daffy about the whole enterprise. Hope triumphing yet again over experience. Thinking it over, the sumo wrestler simile I used earlier was too dignified. What my husband and I most resemble is a pantomime horse. I blush to tell you the haggling that goes into deciding who will play the front end and who the back.

Here Lies My Heart

It is a shrill and misty Manhattan dusk: autumn 1969.
A wan sliver of dying sunlight catches the windows of
the skyscrapers. I am standing furtively at a street corner. Soon my wife emerges from a door across the way.
No—my *ex*-wife. We have been divorced a fortnight,
though I have yet to acknowledge the reality. I have
been waiting here for her; I know she is the psychiatrist's
last client of the afternoon, and that he himself will
sooner or later come out, too. I watch as she drifts away
into the New York manswarm, receding from me like a
pebble in a pond, my college sweetheart. My heart literally palpitates with rage and fear and guilt, all of it so
horrendously vainglorious, yet it is the man I have come
to see, as if merely knowing what he *looks* like might
ease some grievous wrong.

FOR WEEKS I have harbored the vengeful incubus that he and he alone has razed my marriage. That even had she been an ax murderess he would have counseled her, as surely they all did in that histrionic and debilitating American era: "Do what you must to be happy. If it feels good, do it." The *presumption* of him: He is my faceless bête noire, incognito as the great city night, and he has unleashed my most ferocious Confederate tantrums. Frequently have I been tempted to compose for him epistles of nearly Herzogian sweep, have even seriously contemplated what I imposed upon cruel-hearted adults in my small-town Mississippi childhood: gift-wrapped fresh cow manure or dead rats or possums deposited on their front porches in the yuletide.

The mist has turned now into a grim, unhurried rain. Everywhere is the anguished bedlam of the Manhattan Sixties, the panhandlers, the junkies, the crowds so dense that people appear to be standing in queues just to walk down the sidewalks, the staccato clamor of the jackhammers, the steam pouring upward from the sewers as if the world underneath were an inferno, the tall, ominous visage of buildings, so of death, others' and my own. What indeed if someone drops a big mahogany table out a top window and it lands right on me? Such then is my midtown paranoia, real now as my darkest nightmares.

Then, suddenly, he emerges from the same doorway. In stark intuition I know it is he. My heart begins beating fast, and surreptitiously I hasten across the raucous thoroughfare for a closer view. In my anonymous khaki trench coat I could be Gene Hackman tailing the Gallic drug czar down these same streets in *The French Connection.*

I am nearing him now as he pauses at a newsstand in the Gotham ritual of buying the afternoon's *Post,* then the *Village Voice.* I slip into an aperture near a Chock Full O' Nuts and observe him. He is of medium height and wears a gray overcoat. He is young! He looks innocent! He has red hair! This is my final subjugation. I really want him to look like Bernard Malamud. As he walks away I consider moving in on him at the flank, in the manner of Stonewall at Chancellorsville, confronting him nostril to nostril, as Lyndon Johnson did in that day with special antagonists, demanding what arcane knowledge he has appropriated of our joys and sufferings and the things we shared together: the fragrant spring twilights at our university those years ago, the gallant Longhorns whipping the loathsome Aggies, the catfish and beer in the Balcones Hills, the midnight chimes at Oxford, the birth of our child, the old love and promise and hope. Then helplessly I watch as he descends into the steely entrails of the asphalt earth as New Yorkers do, down deep to the rattling IRT, disappearing forever toward whatever cramped Bronx domicile lends him sequester for his cosmic jurisdictions.

ALL THAT was more than twenty years ago, another lifetime really, and during my tenure in the East, nearly three marriages in four were ending in divorce. One summer forenoon in the Hamptons, at a lawn party off a blue and sparkling inlet, I gazed across at the celebrants, some fifty couples I more or less knew from the city: With only two or three exceptions, I was drawn in an instant to note, everyone there had been divorced at least once. Among my contemporaries in those days there seemed a profound desperation about abiding relationships. I searched my friends who had dwelled in the crucible of them for answers, but I found that they knew nothing I did not know. So, as with me, since self-righteousness is surely the mightiest mode of survival, the blame fell on the partner. Everyone was too highly keyed, seething with fickle introspection and aggrandizement. Nothing lasted. It all seemed of a piece with the American Sixties.

She and I were very young when we married, and a very long way too from the East. The Almighty has always been southern in that regard: Get on early with the pristine charter of procreation. One of the clichés of the day held that young marriage was singularly desirable; you would "grow up together," the irony being that growing up can also mean growing apart.

Nonetheless, it survived eleven years, across many terrains, American and otherwise, in good times and bad, and the denouement was terrible, and more than one would ever have bargained for, and the trauma of the ultimate break lasted longer than its duration. The anger, bafflement, jealousy, and sting threatened never to go away, and their scar tissue is probably on my heart forever. Yet whose *fault* was it? I ask myself now, hun-

dreds of miles and a whole generation removed. And
what did it say about ourselves? And what on earth did
it mean? As with many strange and faraway things in
one's life, one wonders, did it ever mean anything at all?

SHE CAME from a raw and sprawling metropolis on
the rise, I from the flatland and canebrakes of deepest
Dixie. I remember as yesterday the first time I ever saw
her. I was playing in a fraternity intramural football
game, and I sighted her on the sidelines talking with
some friends, a stunningly beautiful, dark-complex-
ioned brunette, and she was caught for me in a frieze of
mirthful laughter, and to this day I could show you the
precise spot near the university where we first kissed.
The two of us were important on the campus in those
languid Eisenhower years. I was editor of the student
daily; she was a Phi Beta Kappa and was even elected
"Sweetheart of the University"; five thousand students
sang "The Eyes of Texas" to her in the school gymna-
sium. On my twenty-first birthday she gave me a book
of English verse, and she wrote in it the inscription:

> *Grow old with me,*
> *The best is yet to be,*
> *The last for which the first is made.*

We were married in a chapel in her city, not far from
where she grew up. My father died while we were on
our honeymoon, and I remember the passion and the
grief.

Not many American marriages begin in that Home of Lost Causes, that City of Dreaming Spires—Oxford. I had a scholarship, and to this day I cannot believe we were actually there. There were the impenetrable fogs, the chimes at midnight in the High, always too many bells ringing in the rain. Arm in arm we strolled through the gardens and hidden places of the magical town, reveling in its bleak gray treasures. A wing of an old house was ours, surrounded by lush gardens, the Isis twisting upon itself in the emerald distance. The bachelor Yanks were eternally there, all of them a little in love with her.

On a cold and frosty Christmas Eve, the two of us sat at the high mass in the cathedral of King's College, Cambridge. There was a thin skein of snow on the magnificent sweeping quadrangle outside, and the wonderful stained glass and the elaborate flickering candlelight and the resounding organ and the grand processional in Henry VIII's vaulted chamber, the little English boys in their red ceremonial robes coming ever so slowly down the aisles with their flags and maces, their voices rising, and this was one of the most beautiful things we would ever see in our lives, and we were happy. And then a term break in Paris, and I am walking up Rue Git-le-Coeur, which abuts the Seine, and with the ineffable sights and sounds I conjure Gershwin, and soon there she is, leaning indolently against the upper balcony of our pension, five months pregnant and in a red dress, looking mischievously down at me as I approach, and her sunny words come down through time: "My distinguished husband."

Aᴏᴛᴇʀ ᴛʜᴀᴛ, our heady New York days were suffused with happiness, and then slowly advancing pain. Did the city itself implant the seeds of our own growing recklessness? We were Upper West Side people, back when the Upper West Side was an authentic neighborhood, and at nighttime in the Vietnam years came the echoes of sirens and mayhem from Columbia up the way. On the very day she received her Ph.D. in Bryant Park, Bobby Kennedy was shot.

The fields of fame and ambition grew heavy with pitfalls, though I doubt either of us would have acknowledged that then. Imperceptibly at first, our lives became tense and theatrical—all of celebrity's appurtenances. I was editor of a national magazine, she a young scholar, and our lives converged portentously with the great writers, the critics, the publishers, the millionairesses, the Hollywood heroines, the avatars of the moment's culture: dinner at Clare Booth Luce's or Bennett Cerf's or Punch Sulzberger's, literary celebrations, our photographs in the newsweeklies and newspapers. It happened all too swiftly. In our provincial years our friends thought we would last forever because we were so similar, mainly, I suspect, because we liked books, yet almost against our mutual will we were seeming to become so *different*—had we always been, I wonder, but lacked the experience to see it?—one of us introspective, academic, and disciplined, the other inchoate, nocturnal, uncompromisingly headstrong. How to explain such things, or even to remember them and be honest about them, for memory itself selects and expurgates and diffuses. It was not as fun as it had been.

We bought a farmhouse in the country, even acquired a black Lab puppy to shore up the marriage, and the small-town boy actually joined the anonymous phalanx of Harlem Line commuters in the summer, but the real trouble was just beginning. Doubt is inherent in any reality. She had begun to doubt, and doubt is a contagious hazard, yet the arguments, the insecurities, the melancholies, the insomnias, the inconstancies had to be symptomatic of something deeper, more elusive and mysterious.

All these merged in a daily tangle of hostility and distrust, punctuated by chilly, apprehensive silences. Silence speaks for itself, of course, and there were nights when I did not come home; our precocious love mocked us now, those threads of faded affection seemed frivolous and meaningless, and before our very eyes we had become rivals and antagonists.

The day came when she ordered me from the apartment. Where to go? What to take? I had to escape the city; a confused weekend in Connecticut with friends: "God, you look awful!" The mirror betrayed a complexion sallow as parchment, rings under the eyes like obsidian blisters, and I was developing a wicked little rash about the neck, what we once called *risin's* in Mississippi. Now we were in the deepening maw of divorce, a desolate subterrain all its own. The lawyers, of course, took over—mine a breezy man, cynical and unfeeling, hers hard and professional and unmitigating. Neither she nor I were mavens of heartbreak, and the wound and disarray of "the lawyer phase," as savants of marital rift

chose to call it, were as mean and excruciating as anything I had ever known. I felt I was all beaten up. I feared
I was losing not only my beloved son, but my pride and
dignity, most of my money, my dog, and all the books it
had taken me three years to compensate Blackwell's for.
The nadir came one wintry night in a dark, cold basement apartment I had just rented downtown. The mov-
ers that day had brought a few items of my furniture
there, and the utilities were not working, and by candlelight I rummaged through an ancient bureau that had
once been my great-grandparents', and I found there a
few forlorn mementos of a marriage: letters from her,
even then shriveling at the edges, party invitations, a
menu from the Ile de France, some of our little boy's
toys from Christmases past, a photograph of the two of
us holding him for his first glimpse of the Statue of
Liberty.

It took me a long time to acknowledge she was truly
gone. It was like death, but worse: She was not dead. I
tried diligently to consign her to oblivion, but it did not
work. I still loved her. There descended on my poor betrayed spirit a bizarre, enveloping jealousy, an acid sexual envy, tortured images of her with other men. The
mounting carnage in Vietnam, its headless gluttony and
cataclysm, only reinforced my indulgent fever. After
the divorce I did not see our ten-year-old son for two
months, because I did not trust my bitterness with him,
the things I might say. The first weekend he eventually

came to spend with me, he rang the bell to my apartment, and when I opened the door he stood there with a shopping bag full of gift-wrapped objects. "Hi, Daddy," he said. "I brought you some presents." When I opened them, they turned out to be *my* Sandburg's *Lincoln*, all seven volumes of it, which he had selected to purloin from my own lost library. Was it an act of forgiving? At least I got my Sandburg back.

I became a weekend father. You saw hundreds of these miserable fellow creatures with their offspring on Saturdays in the Central Park Zoo, or F. A.O. Schwarz, or the movie houses along Broadway or Third Avenue, or the old Palisades in Jersey, all trying to be solicitous, as if to make up for something. Many were the Saturdays he and I would spend all day, breakfast to midnight, in Madison Square Garden, never leaving its splendid interior cosmos for so much as a moment: first the bowling alley, then lunch in the Stockyard, then the Knicks in the afternoon for Bradley, Frazier, Reed, and De-Busschere, later a boxing match in the Felt Forum, followed by a comedy act, then dinner all over again in the Stockyard. And when I safeguarded him the next day to a cab on those poignant Sabbath twilights and he left me, I felt unbearably guilty and bereft and alone.

One day he was to meet me in my office at an appointed hour. A good friend, a noted sportswriter, had arranged to take him onto the field at Shea Stadium an hour before a ball game and introduce him to all the Mets and Cardinals. I waited and waited but he did not come. When I telephoned, it was she who answered. I had not cleared the arrangement with her, she said. She was teaching me a lesson. But to meet the *Mets* and *Cards*? I prayed retribution all over again on my bête noire, the shrink. After that I did not talk to or communicate with her for years.

With divorce one gives up a whole way of life—friends, routines, habitudes, commitments. You are on your own again, and in diaphanous territory, and for a while your most fiendish habits may worsen. Then I told myself I could not *afford* to be deranged. I had a demanding job, after all, and scant choice but to function. The problems of real day-to-day life were easier to deal with than the imaginary ones; I willed my own salvation.

For the longest time I thought I could never love again. I was wary and afraid and remembered too much. Yet as the days slowly pass, on into the years, you discover you *can* love again, and that, of course, is a whole other story. But I shudder now to think what my girlfriend of that time had to live with—and not merely the intolerable acrimony and spleen she was forced to share—for in the nature of it we all subconsciously compare our later loves with the first, no matter the wreckage and flaw.

How could I have known then of the psychic hold she would have on me for the rest of my life? The wisps of memory, the dreams, the tender long-ago assurances. Her ghost would exist till I died.

ALL THAT was a very long time ago, and I see now that, as with much of life, this is really a little long-ago

tale of time passing, and of vanished grief. So many of
our friends of those days are dead now, and others have
gone their own way. In the course of an existence,
people move in and out of one's life. Often we do not
know the *whereabouts* of those once dear to us, much less
what they are feeling or remembering. Close relationships oscillate between tranquillity and destruction, between fire and ice. Old fidelities wither, and love dies as
the lovers go on living. There are a few small islands of
warmth and belonging to sustain us if we are lucky. That
is how I wish to think of her now, in the days of our
happiness.

She became a respected feminist and writer. She sub-
sequently married again, to a distinguished man and old
friend. They, too, are now divorced. As for myself, a
writing man, I never remarried, although I came close
two or three times. Was it fear—of love lost, of love renewed?

Yet the further I grew from those painful moments,
the more the bitterness faded; one is left with a kind of
mellowing sadness, and recollections of the beginnings
of love when one was young, the heightened promise
and trust. I also comprehend now that in many ways I
grew and developed into the adult I am today, for better
or worse, because of her, and of her values. Our son is
now older than we were when we married, and I see her
in him, in his courage and commitment.

I sometimes ponder the pain I must have caused *her*,
the selfishness and doubts: *her* side of the matter. Of
course it was not the headshrinker I compelled myself

to pursue that faraway Manhattan dusk, for he was only conduit and symbol. I hope he rewrites Freud and makes a million.

In those inevitable moments of despoiling ill temper, we damage what we cherish. All the time we must somehow grow from the sinews of our own experience, learn to conduct ourselves a little more compassionately—for what is intelligence if not the ability to cope with the recurrences of one's existence?

There remains the incontrovertible burden of lost and damaged love. After all the years we never communicated, now there are random notes of congratulation and remembering. Recently I saw a charming letter she wrote a dear comrade of mine here in the town where I live, and the familiar handwriting leaped out at me in a supple rush, and reminded me of the very best she ever was. Finally, I have learned how difficult love is, how hard to achieve and sustain, no matter who the person or how felicitous the circumstance.

In this moment I find myself driving in a Mississippi Delta twilight toward a warm new love, one that matters to me. All around are the landmarks of my own beginnings, the cypresses in the mossy ponds, the lingering woods, the little hardscrabble towns of my youth, the interminable flatness in the burnt-orange glow. The years are passing, and even in this rare twinkling of serenity and happiness and fulfillment I think of Celia, and remember her.

For Better and Worse

I WAS MARRIED ten years ago, on a brazenly warm day in January, from my father's house, in a dress my mother made, with the same blithe blindness that sends a bungee jumper off a bridge.

I was thirty-four—not a young bride but about right for my narrow slice of the world: baby boomer, middle-class professional, exquisitely self-referential. My kind didn't marry young. In our twenties, marriage was about as hip as Tupperware parties. Driving around in my parents' car the day before the wedding, I felt fever-ish, slightly inauthentic, immensely proud, awkward, and unaware, like a toddler on her maiden voyage as a biped.

I married the man I married because I liked his ver-sion of myself better than my own. I married him be-cause I loved him, because I felt more real with him than

I had felt with anyone else. I'm not sure what, at the time, I meant by *real*. I suppose I was pleased by the person I saw reflected in his eyes. There were a couple of different versions of me in those days: the addled girl in love with the romance of self-destruction and the woman my husband saw, the one who gazed with an archaeologist's interest over the precipice but was in no danger of falling off.

I married him because he loved Ford Madox Ford, because he made the perfect martini, because we could fight and the walls did not fall down, because he was more at home with being a man than any man I knew, because he shouldered responsibility with deceptive ease, and because his eyes welled up with tears elicited by the everyday grace of ordinary people.

They were no better and no worse, as reasons go, than any others I've heard for getting married: Such decisions hinge on a trick of the light, a tick of the clock, the urgent call of an errant and unreliable heart.

I will not be married as long as I thought I would be if the current odds on my husband's lung cancer hold true. I doubt, though everyone tells me I can't know this yet, that I will marry again. I have no plans to commit emotional suttee; I simply cannot imagine how anyone makes the decision to marry a second time, knowing what they know after the first.

MARRIED COUPLES in America now are like punched-out fighters, bathed in each other's sweat, too exhausted to break the clinch, hanging on to each other because it's the only alternative to falling down.

These days, newsmagazines run cover stories worrying about the state of marriage; essayists take bold stands in favor of fidelity. Statistics say marriage is bad for you, at least if you're female: Married women have the worst mental health in the country. (Married men, mirabile dictu, the best.) Talk shows search for scapegoats: feminism, the economy, the government, the mass media, the underclass, the upper class, global warming. On any given weekend, lay ministers and former twelve-steppers are running seminars in dreary, windowless rooms of chain hotels, purportedly teaching people how to stay wed. Even the divorce lawyers are concerned: The American Bar Association now sponsors something called the Preserving Marriages Project.

And yet happy marriage is an accident, as Henry Adams noted. Given the demands of an institution that essentially suggests that you jump into the abyss with a nearby stranger and emerge years later with the core of your being inextricably scrambled with his, it is a wonder not that more marriages don't survive but that more of them don't end in murder.

Still, there's something profoundly threatening to our nervous age about the idea that marriage itself isn't working, as if without it we would have tossed out the last lifeboat. Having exchanged the extended family, the neighborhood bowling league, the two-party system, and the church social for the anonymous camaraderie of the gym and for Prozac's hearty slap on the back, we are down to a nation of two. The state of marriage has become the barometer for measuring the culture's decline, the porousness of its moral fiber.

MARRIAGE IS a bizarre business: a maze, a plot, a prison—a reason to live. It is, for most of us, the narrative spine of our lives, the epic on which we hang our sense of who we are and where we have come from. Marriage is our great American novel.

But we are a people more suited to MTV.

Marriage made sense once. It made sense when it was about money and children. Now marriage is no longer an economic contract but an emotional rip cord, the thing that we hope will land us gently in life, cushion the fall, soften the blows. On it, we stake all our claims to happiness—not the wisest of investment strategies. It is impossible, of course, and yet we persist—out of a still-lambent sense of romance? Or a sheer lack of imagination?

The publishing industry smells the chum in the water: In the past decade, there have been more than 900 books written on the subject of marriage. Pick any point of view, and there is a book to support it: *The End of Marriage; The Good Marriage; Love Between Equals— How Peer Marriage Really Works; Men and Marriage; Tough Marriage: How to Make a Difficult Relationship Work; What to Expect the First Year of Marriage; Intimate Terrorism: The Deterioration of Erotic Life; Together Forever!—125 Loving Ways to Have a Vital and Romantic Marriage.*

The books offer calm reason and logical interpretation; they teach strategy and negotiation. They attempt to protect us from chaos. They offer nice, shiny IKEA [Swedish furniture] marriages, blond wood and clean lines, designed to fit any decor, some assembly required. But a real marriage is a hideous Victorian pile: overstuffed and wildly eccentric, the stains covered with yellowing antimacassars, claw-footed, and in need of a matchbook or two to keep it from tilting. It is a weird blending of obligation and accountability, barbarism and civility. Eventually, it weaves a morality of manners, an intricate pattern of consideration and savagery that only two human beings moving together through time can produce.

THE FIRST Valentine's Day after we were married, my husband gave me bath towels. They were red towels, what are called "seconds"—the kind with snagged threads and other flaws that consign them to the bargain shelves. There was a bow on the shopping bag by way of gift wrapping.

I remember that I cried when I unfolded them. I was furious; the towels were a metaphor that blotted out the sun, shrieked across the reassuring hum of a gradually gathering dailiness. It was a romantic high noon, an emotional and historic accounting in which my husband was found sadly wanting. Now I would say that we were not really married then; we were still in teen-romance mode—he loves me, he loves me not—still riveted by the high drama and pitched emotion of courtship and passion, in which a passing glance can detonate a sudden emotional danger.

What I can't remember anymore is why I was so angry. The reasoning must have been something like this: I have staked everything on this man, and he is not what I thought; he is not the man who cries when he reads Ford Madox Ford. I have defined myself in terms of this choice, this man, and this is the kind of man he is, the Kind Who Gives Towels.

I smile now when I remember this story, set back in the phase when marriage is still a mirror, reflecting back only one's carefully constructed, easily shattered conceit. Now my husband gives me bath towels every Valentine's Day, and every Valentine's Day I laugh. It has become part of our mythology. But the laughter is its own edgy commentary on how things have changed, how we have changed each other, how the two people who smile at this joke are indelibly stained with each other's expectations and disappointments, how who we are is a composite of who we might have been refracted through the lens of whom we married. The laughter is a counterpane, covering the lumps we've dealt each other, the scars left from the various surgeries we've performed on each other, the enthusiasms dampened so that a couple might emerge.

MY HUSBAND was married when I met him. He and his wife had been together for fifteen years; they had three children. I mention this because even now it is hard for me to reconcile the person I thought I was with the person who could wreak so much havoc in other lives. My comfort had always been that the only one who got smashed up in my accidents was me. So now, despite all the time and talk and reconciliation, the ways in which his children are so dear to me, the ways in which his ex-wife and I are embedded in each other's lives, there is a bitter sense of justice that the catastrophe that is happening, is happening on my watch. I earned this karmic crash.

I married him. And then I thought, Now what? I didn't know this story. I didn't know what was supposed to happen next. The plots available to us are so thin: We were happy until . . . she got the promotion, he met the other woman, the children went into detox. The stories that end happily are thinner still. For years, when I was single, I kept tacked to my office bulletin board a photograph of a couple in frozen ecstasy, whirling each other around at their fiftieth-anniversary party, the look of a mad, glad girl on her ancient face, the grin of the skull on his. They scared me, the way they were locked in their fossilized notion of love. I kept it as a warning: Don't let this happen to you. Last summer, I watched an old couple walk hand in hand down the beach a good, long while—pink, doughy flesh in T-shirts and shorts, the children's clothes we all wear made pitiable now by the body's comic fall. They looked happy. I thought about the strings that come attached to answered prayers.

Television permanently distorted the popular idea of marriage. The sitcom wiped out the essential eccentricity of such unions, the odd Mendelian experiments that grow and twist themselves into fantastic shapes in the privacy of the bedroom and other dark arenas of the psyche; instead, it gave us pale paradigms to emulate, Ward and June Cleaver. (Lucy and Ricky got closer to the truth—there were between the Ricardos draconian ultimatums and deceptions, manic rows and thwarted ambitions—but then, that was meant to be slapstick.)

On TV, marriage, like God, was eternal. At the turn of the century, the departure of the last child from the domestic nest coincided with the death of one of the spouses, but sitcoms never acknowledged the inconvenient fact that modern longevity had taken away the traditional cure for many an unhappy marriage.

Even without a nudge from mortality, John Updike saw a life cycle in a marriage: "That a marriage ends is less than ideal," he wrote in the preface to *Too Far to Go*. "But all things end under heaven, and if temporality is held to be invalidating, then nothing real succeeds."

We seem unable to tolerate such hard truths in the nineties, in this nation of micromanagers, where parents-to-be hire experts to plot the most advantageous month in which to conceive their offspring. According to a University of Washington study, even marriage can now be subjugated to an equation—the researchers claimed that they could "actually quantify the ratio of positive to negative interactions needed to maintain a marriage in good shape." They found that "satisfied couples, no matter how their marriages stacked up against the ideal, were those who maintained a five-to-one ratio of positive to negative moments." Ladies and gentlemen, get out your calculators.

It seems as if we are trying to talk ourselves into something, like urbanites onto the farm or sybarites into the sermon. Now that nostalgia is our highest art form, marriage has become another vanished dream to be resurrected back into the thing it never was.

The late philosopher-curmudgeon Christopher Lasch cast a cold eye on our current attitudes. To his mind, the rise of a managerial and professional elite—experimental in its values, disdainful of tradition, transient and unencumbered—has shattered the sorts of standards that make institutions like marriage viable. This new elite, this meritocracy, lacks such basic marital assets as loyalty, a sense of responsibility for one's actions, and pride of place, Lasch wrote.

Okay, guilty, guilty, guilty. We are too smart and too rich—and also too stupid—to stay married to each other for life. So why do we watch in horror, gawkers at a traffic accident, when a marriage breaks up?

Because marriage has become the coin of our personal happiness, which makes it a savage business.

W HEN I was single, I equated marriage with drowning: Your identity disappeared, your privacy was invaded, your self submerged. After I married, I found out that I was right; what I hadn't known was how much of an amphibian I could be.

It is early in our marriage. My husband and I are at a dinner party. It is one of the first we have attended together, so we have not yet worked out our public persona, the two-headed vaudeville act all married couples become in other people's living rooms. We have not yet developed the group of people who will become our friends.

This time, we happen to be at a table surrounded by mine. I am very nervous, and because I am very nervous and like to drink, I drink too much. The Jack Daniel's makes me long for a Camel. The cigarette is a talisman, a declaration of allegiance to my own self, and although I officially gave up smoking several years ago, I enjoy the throaty rape of the smoke with an immoderate, illicit pleasure.

Late in the evening, I look down the table from the warm interior of some prolonged fit of liquor-enhanced laughter to see my husband's cold, unsmiling face. I know the look on his face. It is the look that says, This is not the Woman Who Loves Schubert's String Quintet in C. This is the woman my wife warned me about, the Tacky Little Floozy Who Will Ruin My Life. Without saying another word to me, my husband leaves the table and drives home, leaving me to find my own way back.

My self-indulgence, my lack of restraint, he tells me later, has disappointed him. I bridle, not seeing that his anger obscures his fear that he really has stepped onto a runaway train. I see only the way in which I have become the flawed reflection of his self-esteem. Are we really now meant to be mirrors of each other? Does every public thing we do raise or lower our sense of ourselves in the world accordingly?

The answer, I learned in time, was yes, of course. Married couples are hybrids, forced blooms, and we make ungainly composites in the beginning, molting in public, like transsexuals before the knife but after the hormone treatments have begun.

It is an unnatural way to live, but that is not necessarily a bad thing. The quiet fund of conspiracy, the shared opinions and the shared visions—"Their eyes," Updike wrote, "had married and merged to three"—begin to accumulate weight and meaning. Over the years, the dry wit and the dumb jokes and the occasional blinding beauty of another soul make things like abrupt departures and stolen cigarettes not worth the fight. Maybe marriage isn't the great civilizer conservative pontificators want it to be, but at least it is a medium—a theater for our incivility.

MARRIAGES, after all, begin in delusions, in the drug of love, in a lie—if not knowing who you are and who the other one is can be called a lie. In the Richard Yates novel *Revolutionary Road*, a wife reflects on how a boy she liked to kiss after he walked her home from a party became her husband: "The only real mistake, the only wrong and dishonest thing, was ever to have seen him as anything more than that. Oh, for a month or two, just for fun, it might be all right to play a game like that with a boy; but all these years! And all because, in a sentimentally lonely time long ago, she had found it easy and agreeable to believe whatever this one particular boy felt like saying, and to repay him for that pleasure by telling easy, agreeable lies of her own, until each was saying what the other most wanted to hear—until he was saying, 'I love you' and she was saying, 'Really, I mean it; you're the most interesting person I've ever met.' What a subtle, treacherous thing it was to let yourself go that way!"

All marriages begin in myth. The myth is the carapace under which the real marriage takes shape; the cracking of the carapace, like the breakup of the ice on a spring-swollen river, is a deafening thing. In our case, the original myth was all the stronger because of the destruction its creation had occasioned. Since we had plundered one marriage to make another, our particular myth, the romance of two souls so made for each other that the claims of no one could stand in their way, gave way only reluctantly to the reality of daily life. You do not break up a marriage only to argue over the dishes with the one who was meant to take you away from the exasperating dullness of arguing over the dishes.

We fought, we skinned our knees, we tasted the poison in each other.

All marriages are mended garments. In marriage, you don't make it all better; you get over it. By marrying, Robert Louis Stevenson warned, "you have willfully introduced a witness into your life . . . and can no longer close the mind's eye upon uncomely passages, but must stand up straight and put a name upon your actions." Be-cause if you don't, she will.

"Every major argument has a cost, a potential parting of the ways, when you can say, That's it, it's over," says a friend who has been married for seventeen years. "Then you think, I can't shut down my whole life, and you don't, but there's a price, an unhappiness that gets woven in, and you deal with it. Some drink, some mope, some get religious, some have affairs. But if you leave, you could lose a lot that you value. What if you married a second time and were just as unhappy? Marriage isn't a tradable commodity; it's an element you live in."

I remember after one of our early rows, my husband and I emerged into the light of the afternoon to look at an apartment we had an appointment to see. The woman renting the place stared at me quizzically. She was trying to place me, and in time she did: It turned out that she was my ex-boyfriend's ex-wife. She and I laughed uneasily over the coincidence, but my husband was visibly shaken by the breathtaking fragility of hu-man arrangements. We both felt the windows rattle; I could see it was the first time he had considered the idea that we might not be together forever. I think for a time we treated each other more carefully after that, having become more aware of the tremors beneath our feet.

My wife is becoming less interested in me," a friend tells me over lunch. He says this with calm dispassion, as if describing the migrating habits of geese. "What I don't think she expected is how much like my father I would turn out to be." And he? Is he less interested in her? "What's surprising to me still is the things you don't know, the ways in which the other remains a stranger to you. That's disappointing, because there was once a sense that you could talk about anything, that you would tell each other everything." But that, he says, was "back in the time when you could be honest without being hurtful," back before the power plays made every observation a criticism, every criticism a hand grenade.

We put each other on leashes; we use the leashes like whips. The leashes vary from couple to couple: I have a friend whose husband has insisted that she avoid short skirts because, he says, her legs aren't good enough. On the other hand, she goes off to Paris every year by herself for ten days' R & R, and he doesn't blink twice. I wear what I want to wear, but if I were to propose such a trip to Paris, both my husband and I would consider the idea tantamount to a divorce decree. We are each accountable to the other, and that accountability is both the best and worst part of marriage. It keeps you sane. It also drives you crazy.

Five years into our marriage, we are living in New York. Things have changed. We are no longer the scandalous couple of the small-town gossip mill of Washington, D.C. I am no longer the ingenue. My husband is no longer the keeper of all my aspirations. New York dazzles me: Unbound from the round of decorous Beltway dinner parties, I become restless, ready for something new. The fights grow bitter. I want a child and he does not. Our myth is cracking. Privately, I think, we both pull out a set of scales, begin to wonder if what we have given up is worth what we got. There are nights when we sit by the dinner table with nothing to say to each other, and I remember all the nights in restaurants when I have watched such silence between other couples with smug contempt, wondering how they ever got that way.

My husband goes on a trip, for six weeks, to Africa. For the first time in a long while, I am completely alone. Before long, I am deep into adultery: I take a long walk at night in the rain, exulting in the fact that there is no one waiting for me at home, aggrieved and wanting dinner; I spend an afternoon listening to Linda Ronstadt, a singer my husband hates, while knitting, an activity he finds ridiculously mindless. In the morning, I open the refrigerator and drink orange juice straight from the carton, a habit that I have concealed since I saw him wince when he caught me in the act. In social settings, on my own now, not part of a couple, I haul out my old camouflage—taunting, flirtatious, argumentative, the persona I adopted when I was single. It's a bit tattered here and there, but it still works.

I am having, I realize, an affair with myself. It is an innocent adultery, as these things go, but it still feels like a betrayal—of the person I am with my husband, the one who represents my half of the couple.

When my husband returns, I am glad to see him and relieved that I am glad, that my life is simply better with him in it. We are interesting to each other again. But now there is this being, folded up again in my back pocket, this doppelgänger, the person I might have been had I not married. She worries me.

There are cycles to this domestic life—times when you're in love; times when you coexist as amiable roommates, too busy to take much notice of each other as long as the domestic machinery is humming along; times, too, when the air becomes too thin for you to breathe, the walls between you as translucent as membrane when what you want is good, thick concrete.

I think that is when the bickering begins. The sharp tone to the casual comment, the stubborn refusal to give in, are the holes we puncture in the top of the lid to make sure enough air gets in.

A friend of mine, recently divorced, is sitting in our living room after dinner. We are talking about Tiananmen Square, a subject I know nothing about, unlike my husband, the former foreign editor of two major newspapers. We are not discussing the righteousness of the current foreign policy toward China. We are tangling over some perfectly meaningless point of fact. We cover the same rocky patch of ground for several interminable minutes while some still-sane remnant of my character wonders why it is so important that I win this argument.

I look at my friend, the survivor of a cruel marriage and a crueler divorce. She is smiling. I ask her why. "I just remembered why I'm not married anymore," she says.

In the cancer ward, my husband is dozing. In the next

bed lies an elderly man, dry as parchment. His wife sits next to him, their two voices topping each other, the incessant ballet of mosquitoes.

"I told you to call her."

"You never mentioned it."

"I just thought it would be better for you, that's all."

"Me? You were thinking of me? Since when have you thought about me?"

Love me. Leave me alone. Love me. Remember that once you loved me. Love me. But never forget that you will never know me. There was something oddly reassuring about their voices, about the insect dance in that stern white room, dailiness among the IV tubes, a talisman against the day when one of the voices stops.

Every marriage has a story, says a friend of mine, a plot twist, "a critical moment that changes things, like a tree after a bad storm, the event that colored their whole lives—Bill had to go to war; we lost the money when the market crashed. So that where you end up is not where you began, which is both the heaven and the hell of marriage. You are not who you were and she is not who she was, and the balance on any given day, of whether that is a good or a bad thing, shifts precariously."

My marriage assumed its final form on a day in April laced in green when my husband walked to a lectern in a Washington church and delivered the eulogy for his twelve-year-old and only son.

He talked about his son's short life, and at the end he

asked the congregation to say the boy's name out loud together one last time. And all that I know about love and courage and timeless sorrow I learned from looking at his face as he listened while we did as he asked.

I sat in a pew with the boy's mother, whose strength and generosity still astound me, and his two sisters, my stepdaughters, just entering their own spring. Around us was a force of people who had buoyed this family and kept them afloat for a terrible week and would continue to do so in the years ahead. This was the community in which my husband and I had taken our place together.

I knew many of their stories: Some of these people were pompous and proud, some dull and stingy with their affection, others gaudy in their ambition, a few un-recognized in their goodness. But that day, it wasn't their foibles that caught the light; it was the immense, tangled net of them, the strength of that net, the weight it could support. The terrible necessity of other people at last came home to me.

My husband and I would never be the same after what happened to his son. The moment when I understood the horror and the beauty of that fact, the way in which we had been changed, the way in which our knowledge of each other was unfathomably deepened, the way in which we were inextricably a part of each other, was the moment when I felt I finally knew what it meant to be married.

IN LIFE, Updike wrote, "There are four forces: love, habit, time, and boredom. Love and habit at short range are immensely powerful, but time, lacking a minus charge, accumulates inexorably, and with its brother boredom levels all."

My married friends and I talk about adultery sometimes. Late at night, on the rare evenings we are up late at night, or on the phone, on the more frequent afternoons when we are avoiding the things we have to do, we discuss the weirdness of the idea that we will never make love to anyone new. Implicit in the conversations is the idea that none of us have.

At one late-night dinner party, the question on the table is what constitutes adultery, where we draw the line. Drunken kissing in a taxicab? An out-of-town blow job? We are goosing ourselves a little, wondering what we would do, wondering which of us have done it.

The single people at the table regard us sternly. The merest kiss is adultery, they tell us. They have much to learn. They think adultery is about sex.

Not all of us find adultery an interesting question—there is one participant in the conversation who insists that he would rather eat an olive than make love. It is a sensible attitude, and I envy him to the same degree to which he astonishes me. I prefer his position to the rather smug and priggish new piety about adultery to be found these days—we are all too busy, too tired, too well adjusted, the theory goes, to indulge in that sort of thing. According to this line of thinking, adultery is a syndrome like alcohol addiction, a kink in the family genes. Or adultery is quaint, something people did in the fifties instead of watching pay-per-view.

But the fact is, adultery is always an issue, an insistent tongue seeking out the sore tooth. Marriage demands virtue, but virtue is an amputation, and what is lost is one of the things that make one feel most alive. Desire is such an anarchic state, so perfectly heedless, that it doesn't have much to do with morality or guilt or virtue or innocence and shouldn't have to answer to any such judgments. But there is no way to reconcile the satisfactions of abiding love with the leap your heart takes when you're touching someone you have thought about touching for a long, long time.

There is a depth of intimacy to domesticated lovemaking that nothing can equal; yet there are times when the idea of making love to just one person for the rest of your life can make your head hurt. So where does that leave us, apart from staring at the ceiling at three o'clock in the morning or at each other over the remnants of the tiramisu? I don't know. Marriage, when it works, is a mystery made up of such a complicated ebb and flow of affection, admiration, fury, ritual, and gradually unfolding understanding that with the right person it's not a bad way to live a life. But if it means giving up fire and first kisses, then it seems like more than a little death. So one is left with a simple choice: self-denial or betrayal, contentment or ecstasy, earth or fire, the lady or the tramp.

Most of us choose not to take the risk while leaving open the loophole, in much the same way that I continue not to smoke only because I pretend that I haven't smoked my last cigarette. But in the end, adultery—real, old-fashioned sex with someone else—is a fairly stupid issue: One of the best marriages I know, one in which the levels of sanity and self-respect, consideration and camaraderie, are reassuringly high, involves a couple for whom the judicious use of the extramarital affair has seen each of them through an extended siege of the other's craziness. I've seen totally faithful marriages for which the only sensible solution is a nice murder-suicide.

For most of us, adultery is a gauge to the stage and status of our marriage. Most of us sitting around the table are at an awkward age, too old to consider ourselves young, too young to consider ourselves old. Our preoccupation with the subject is in part a generational legacy: The ecstatic abandon of Woodstock is the benchmark against which we measure ourselves. Unlike people now in their twenties, who grew up in a harder school and know a good deal when they see one, we were not after contentment but cliff-hangers. The past ten years has seen a surge in what are now called "starter" marriages, as ephemeral as spring. My tribe settled for living together. We got around to marriage late and cautiously, perhaps too late ever to achieve the kind of seamless duality where the border of one personality bleeds inconspicuously into the other.

For us, then, adultery is a metaphor for what's been given up, the existential quality of experience, the random act, the assertion of privacy and independence. Its promise is protection against the kind of cold comfort that Edith Wharton's protagonist in *The Age of Innocence* nurses after giving up the woman he loves for the woman he has promised to marry: "Their long years together had shown him that it did not so much matter if marriage was a dull duty, as long as it kept the dignity of a duty: lapsing from that, it became a mere battle of ugly appetites."

We have no modern affinity for the Edwardian sense of sacrifice as an endorphin high. Marriage has a dangerous relationship with happiness; it was meant to be measured in terms of economic necessity, not by the yardstick of capitalism. "As soon as [men and women] introduce into their private life a sort of inarticulate system of cost accounting—they cannot fail to become aware of the heavy personal sacrifices that family ties and especially parenthood entail under modern conditions," wrote the economist Joseph Schumpeter in 1942.

On the other hand, adultery is at best a stopgap measure. We need other, more contemporary answers to the dry rot that sets in, to the slow, insidious accretions of acid and lethal insight that a lifetime's—or even the prospect of a lifetime's—accumulation of microscopic observations yields. Surprisingly, the Republican radicals in Congress may have come up with the solution for what ails marriages. It's simple, it's facile, it's pragmatic in the superficial way today's politics demands. The answer to marriage's downward spiral is the same as their answer to congressional inertia and unresponsiveness: term limits.

Instead of getting married for life, men and women (in whatever combination suits their sexual orientation) should sign up for a seven-year hitch. If, at the end of those seven years, they want to reenlist for another seven, they may do so. But after that, the marriage is over. Those who wish to stay together after that may live in what used to be called sin. There would be minor penalties; such flouting of the law might be a misdemeanor, akin to smoking dope.

Such penalties would naturally lead to some inconvenience, but on the other hand there would be the rush of illicitness, a whiff of disapprobation to long-term cohabitation that could jazz things up considerably. Other benefits are obvious: No more stigma attached to the children of divorced parents; all marriages would end equally. No more divorce lawyers. No more fiftieth-wedding-anniversary parties to attend.

After the seven or fourteen years, one could move on—to another marriage, perhaps, but maybe to something less restrictive. The ex-hippie in me says that it should be possible after marriage to evolve to a higher plane, to living arrangements involving ex-lovers, best friends, children, stray cats, and green plants that create the sweet rhythms of domestic life we look for in marriage while allowing room for the barbed-wire frontiers necessary for adult sanity.

But the realist in me remembers that there is no way you are going to put up with another person's predilection for unwashed dishes or Frank Sinatra unless you are inextricably entwined with the perpetrator, both physically and financially. So I think we're probably stuck with marriage, even if what you end up with is the pride of the survivor, that the two of you weathered the storm, that you still cherish the person and all he has meant to you. Even if what you end up with is the conclusion a friend of mine came to: "I still can't imagine being happier," he says. "I just didn't realize how unhappy I could become."

M EMORY IS a slut, open to any interpretation. I live in three time zones these days—past, present, and future. I think about the person I was before I married and worry that the demons in her will come back to haunt me. I think about the future only when it slips in the unexpected stiletto: Wobbling about on rented skates, scanning the crowd for my five-year-old daughter, I see a man sitting at a table. From the back, he looks a little like my husband. There is a rush of fond surprise and then a chill. I imagine making the same mistake in later years, when it is not followed by the recollection that my husband is, in fact, at home.

Terminal illness and lack of time perform a Khmer Rouge–like obliteration on the dull lacquer of years. There are moments when my husband and I are back in the year one, and all the reasons we fell in love are so apparent, the barnacles of grievance and irritation removed so completely, that I become furious with marriage for the way it buries love in the sludge of who takes out the trash, the way routine replaces romance.

But then it is a Sunday afternoon. My husband and I are playing Monopoly Junior with our daughter. Chet

Baker's trumpet fills the room. I hated jazz when I was single, but now our marriage is steeped in this music, in the ways I have changed and the things I've come to know, in exasperation and elegance, in the poetry of dailiness, in the solace of each other's company. I see the ways my husband saved me, the ways I saved him. There is still pain in the phantom limbs lost in the making of this marriage, but in that moment the loss seems a manageable part of the trade. I see only the courage and kindness that marriage elicits, not the cost, and it seems to me that it gives us our only chance to be heroes. I want the song Baker is playing never to end.

I don't think anyone chooses to be a hero, not after they know the price to be paid. I know I don't want to be changed again, to be blended, smoothed, to pare down the sharp ends of my personality to fit into the too-small allowances made for them. But I look at who I was and who I am, and I want to be nowhere except where I am now, even though, and perhaps because, I know it is the one thing I will not be given. And while the song is playing, I know that, yes, I would marry again, if I could simply marry the very same man.

Credits

Contributors

JOEL ACHENBACH is a reporter for *The Washington Post* and the author of *Why Things Are: Answers to Every Essential Question in Life* (1991), *Why Things Are: The Big Picture, Vol. 2* (1993), and *Why Things Are and Why Things Aren't: The Answers to Life's Greatest Mysteries* (1996).

AMY BLOOM's collection of short stories *Come to Me* (1994) was nominated for both the National Book Award and the Los Angeles Times First Fiction Award. Her stories and articles have appeared in *The New Yorker, Story, Antaeus, River City, Room of One's Own, Vogue,* and other fiction magazines in the United States and abroad. Ms. Bloom has been a contributing editor for *New Woman* and *Self* magazines. Her critically acclaimed novel, *Love Invents Us* (1997), has been sold in Brazil, Germany, Israel, the Netherlands, and the United Kingdom. She is currently working on a new collection of short stories.

LEWIS BUZBEE is the author of *Fliegelman's Desire* (1990), a novel. His work has appeared in *Harper's, GQ, Paris Review, The Best American Poetry* series, and elsewhere. "This Is My Last Affair" is from a forthcoming memoir *The Other Man: Diary of an Affair.*

LYNN DARLING is a former contributing editor to *Esquire* magazine.

LOUISE DESALVO is the author of *Breathless: An Asthma Journal* (1997), *Vertigo: A Memoir* (1996), and co-editor of *Territories of the Voice: Contemporary Stories by Irish Women Writers* (1991). She is currently working on a book about adultery. She is a professor of English at Hunter College, and lives in Teaneck, NJ.

MARK DOTY is the author of five books of poetry, including *My Alexandria* (1993) and most recently, *Sweet Machine* (1998). He has also written a memoir, *Heaven's Coast* (1996). His work has received the National Book Critics Circle Award, the T. S. Eliot Prize, the PEN/Martha Albrand Prize for Nonfiction, and other honors. He lives in Provincetown, Massachusetts, and Houston, Texas, where he teaches at the University of Houston.

GERALD EARLY is a professor of English and Director of the African and Afro-American Studies Program at Washington University in St. Louis. He is the author of *The Culture of Bruising: Essays on Prizefighting, Literature, and Modern American Culture* (1994), a nominee for the National Book Critics Circle Award in Criticism.

BARBARA EHRENREICH writes and speaks about social and political issues, and contributes to many magazines, such as *The Nation* and *Mother Jones*. Her books include *The Snarling Citizen* (1995), *The Worst Years of Our Lives: Irreverent Notes from a Decade of Greed* (1990), *The Hearts of Men: American Dreams and the Flight from Commitment* (1983), and *Witches, Midwives, and Nurses: A History of Women Healers* (1973), co-authored with Deirdre English.

CAL FUSSMAN and his wife recently celebrated their sixth wedding anniversary with their two children. He writes a monthly column for *Esquire* called "The Perfect Man."

VIVIAN GORNICK'S latest book, *The End of the Novel of Love* (1997), was a finalist for the National Book Critics Circle Award. She has been acclaimed for her books of memoir, *Fierce Attachments* (1987) and *Approaching Eye Level* (1996) and a book of criticism, *Essays in Feminism* (1978). She lives in New York City.

CYNTHIA HEIMEL is a former columnist for the *Village Voice*, a token feminist at *Playboy* magazine, a contributor to *The New York Times*, and a contributing editor at *Vogue*. Her play *A Girl's*

Guide to Chaos (1988) has been performed in Los Angeles, Chicago, New York, and all around the country. Her books include *When Your Phone Doesn't Ring, It'll Be Me* (1996), *Get Your Tongue Out of My Mouth, I'm Kissing You Goodbye* (1994), *If You Can't Live Without Me, Why Aren't You Dead Yet?* (1992), and *Sex Tips for Girls* (1983). She lives in Los Angeles.

AMY HEMPEL is the author of *Tumble Home* (1997), *Reasons to Live* (1995), and *At the Gates of the Animal Kingdom* (1990), and is the co-editor of *Unleashed: Poems by Writers' Dogs* (1995). Her stories are widely anthologized in the United States and abroad and have appeared in such magazines as *Harper's, Vanity Fair,* and *The Quarterly.* She teaches in the Graduate Writing Program at Bennington College and lives in New York City.

EDWARD HOAGLAND's sixteenth book, *Tigers and Ice,* appeared this year. His previous books include *Balancing Acts* (1993), *Heart's Desire* (1991), *The Snow Leopard* (1987), *African Calliope: A Journey to the Sudan* (1981), and *Notes from the Century Before: A Journal from British Columbia* (1969). He teaches at Bennington College.

MARJORIE INGALL, a former senior writer at *Sassy* magazine, is the author of *The Field Guide to North American Males* (1997). She has written for *Ms., Mademoiselle, Wired, Food & Wine,* and *The San Francisco Examiner.* Her hair is no longer purple.

KATE JENNINGS is a writer living in New York. She has published several books of poetry, essays, and short stories in Australia. *Snake* (1997), a novel, is her first book published in the United States.

PHILLIP LOPATE is the author of *Portrait of My Body: Personal Essays* (1996) and editor of *The Anchor Essay Annual 1997* and *The Art of the Personal Essay: An Anthology from the Classical Era to the Present* (1994).

NANCY MAIRS is the author of several books, including *Waist-High in the World: A Life among the Nondisabled* (1997), *Ordinary*

Time: Cycles in Marriage, Faith, and Renewal (1994), *Voice Lessons: On Becoming a (Woman) Writer* (1994), and *Carnal Acts: Essays* (1990). She teaches at the University of Arizona at Tucson.

DAVID MAMET is the author of *The Cryptogram, Oleanna*, and *Glengarry Glen Ross*, among other plays, as well as *Make-Believe Town: Essays and Remembrances* (1996) and the novel *The Village* (1996). His screenplays include *The Untouchables, The Verdict, The Spanish Prisoner*, and *House of Games*.

WILLIE MORRIS is the author of several books, including *My Dog Skip* (1995), *New York Days* (1994), and *The Last of the Southern Girls* (1994).

KATHA POLLITT is the author of a book of poetry, *Antarctic Traveller* (1982), and *Reasonable Creatures: Feminism and Society in American Culture at the End of the Twentieth Century* (1994). She writes a column for *The Nation*, "Subject to Debate," and lives in New York City.

REBECCA WALKER is the founder of Third Wave Direct Action Corporation, a national nonprofit organization devoted to cultivating young women's leadership and activism. She has been a contributing editor to *Ms.* since 1989 and is the editor of *To Be Real: Telling the Truth and Changing the Face of Feminism.* She is currently at work on a book of autobiographical nonfiction entitled *Morphology: Memoir of a Shifting Self* and an anthology on bisexuality, *Having Our Cake*, both forthcoming from Riverhead Books. She lives in Los Angeles.

ACKNOWLEDGMENT

Many thanks to Marya Van't Hul, my dear friend and colleague, without whom this book would not exist.

D.C.